POWER
BANKERS

POWER BANKERS

SALES CULTURE SECRETS OF HIGH-PERFORMANCE BANKS

MICHAEL F. PRICE

JOHN WILEY & SONS, INC.
New York • Chichester • Brisbane • Toronto • Singapore

Copyright © 1992 by Michael F. Price

Published by John Wiley & Sons, Inc.

Library of Congress Cataloging-in-Publication Data

Price, Michael F.
    Power bankers : sales culture secrets of high performance banks /
by Michael F. Price.
        p.   cm.
    Includes bibliographical references and index.
    ISBN 0-471-55555-X
    1. Bank marketing.   I. Title.
HG1616.M3P75   1992
332.1′068′8—dc20   91-35803
                                                                    CIP

Printed in the United States of America.
10 9 8 7 6 5 4 3 2 1
Printed and bound by Malloy Lithographing, Inc.

With Special Thanks . . .

This book is dedicated to all the banking professionals that I have had the pleasure and honor of working with, to my colleagues at RMA who believe in the future of banking as much as I do, to Philip Kotler whose kind letter of support inspired the completion of this book, and to Janice Osdoby and Jack Collins whose one pervasive question, "How?" led to this project.

I am also very grateful to Dick Butler, Peter Conway, Terri Gillis, Philip Goldsmith, Barrie Graham, Wendy Grau, Harry Howell, John Krout, George McCullagh, Dennis Piggott, Harry Prenger, John Russell, and Rob Ward; they reviewed the initial manuscript and their thoughts and comments were invaluable.

Special acknowledgement is also due the staff of the BMA (Chicago), ABA library (Washington), CIB (London), Harvard Business School Baker Library (Cambridge), BAI (Chicago), and the Advisory Board (Washington) whose research facilities, publications, and assistance added immeasurably to the content of this book.

Last, I would like to thank my best friend, partner, and wife Lydia, whose support and encouragement made this book possible.

Preface

Building a high-performance sales culture has been an elusive goal for many bank executives. A successful sales culture depends on implementing a whole series of concepts, few of which have been written about extensively or in any one source. Although many books have probed the sales process, few have focused on *building a sales culture* and none contains the "hands-on," leading-edge concepts needed to create a high-performance sales culture.

This book is the result of more than three years of research, and meetings with over 250 prominent banks. *Power Bankers* is a collection of implementable ideas taken from a number of banks, ranging in size from the largest global money-center banks to small, highly profitable community banks. This book provides bank executives with an arsenal of more than 200 original ideas and tools, each of which can be readily implemented with proven results.

The term "wholesale banking" in the context of this book encompasses everything other than retail banking (that is, commercial lending, corporate finance, institutional trust, etc.). The term "relationship manager" describes all customer contact officers (both wholesale and retail), unless otherwise specified. Check-off boxes are provided in front of each concept for marking as you read. You are challenged to assess which concepts would be useful to you, and implement those ideas that will improve your bank's sales culture and performance.

One of Tom Peters's few regrets after having written *In Search of Excellence* was the citing of specific corporate names in his book. He found that readers focused on the companies themselves rather than on the concepts being presented. This book makes a deliberate effort to avoid such shortcomings by not specifying bank names. However, I am deeply indebted to those bankers and consultants who shared with me their strategies, tactics, and trade secrets. Without them, this book would not have been possible.

MICHAEL F. PRICE

P.S. To receive notification of future editions, updates, related books, and supplements, simply return a photocopy of the registration page at the end of this book.

Contents

Contents

Contents

Contents

Contents

Contents

List of Tables and Figures

1

Introduction and Goals

Overcapacity has far outdistanced the expanding global market for financial services. Until this excess banking capacity corrects itself through the laws of supply and demand, there will exist a Darwinian environment in which only the strongest and most adaptable banks will succeed. To survive, most banks will continue to transform their sources of revenue, ultimately becoming much more dependent on niche markets, fee-based income, technology, and transaction services income. Now, more than ever before, the importance of enhancing both revenues and margins is crucial as the financial services industry implosion continues. Whether the strategic intent is to preserve or increase margins or market share, an advanced sales culture will play a vital role.

Although most bankers readily acknowledge the contribution of a true sales culture toward bank profitability, building a sales culture that is both effective and self-sustaining has been a slow and difficult process. Despite these obstacles, most banks have examined and then implemented strategies to develop sales cultures, in order to become more competitive. Banks that have instituted these first-generation sales cultures have experienced varying degrees of success.

This book provides innovative, adoptable ideas that have

proven to be successful in those banks with high-performance sales cultures. Since it is assumed that a culture is actually the combination of many subcultures, this book will dissect the organization, providing usable strategies and tools at all levels, from the chief executive officer to the line manager. The ideas presented, when implemented jointly, will foster a high-performance, second-generation sales culture.

The essence of competitive strategy is to initiate advantages faster than competitors can imitate existing ones. Market opportunities available today will not exist tomorrow. When opportunity is identified, it must be seized and acted on with immediacy and strategic purpose. Each of us is in a position, regardless of how large or small, to make a difference. You are challenged to read the ideas in this book, seize the opportunity, and transform your team into *Power Bankers*.

As capital markets have continued to develop, many corporate financial managers have been able to bypass commercial banks and tap the capital markets directly, thus eliminating the need to borrow from banks and effectively reducing the firms' cost of capital. As the development of capital markets spreads globally, the lending role of banks will continue to decrease, eventually depending primarily on middle-market, small-business, and retail borrowers for traditional interest income. As industry finds itself less dependent on commercial banks for capital, a global surplus of banks has developed. Banks not able to adapt successfully to rapidly changing market conditions, or not insulated from market forces by way of niche strategies, will cease to exist as separate entities.

Community and rural bankers serving remote markets often find it difficult to see how international competition affects their markets and profitability. Yet, at this very moment, other not-so-distant banks are evaluating the markets that these community bankers take for granted. Signs of global competition in niche locations and markets will materialize in the form of increased competition from other aggressive domestic banks due to earnings pressure and strategic advantage deterioration in their own traditional markets. Overcapacity is tangible and affects *every* bank—globally and without exception.

To remain viable in the long term, a bank must create a sustainable competitive advantage. Such an advantage can be developed by being the lowest-cost producer (unlikely, in most cases), becoming a market leader by creating preferable new products before competitors imitate existing products (doubtful, except for small product "enhancements"), or by surpassing competitors in terms of sales and service within selected target markets. The latter is by far the most feasible strategy for most banks. Unfolding a highly evolved *second-generation* sales culture is the natural outcome of a bank's pursuit of a sustainable competitive advantage.

Building such a sales culture involves much more than ensuring that employees can sell a service to a customer. In high-performance banks, selling describes building a relationship in which the customer will consistently prefer to use the bank's services over other alternatives. Selling does more than describe the business development steps and initial contact necessary to make a customer acquisition; selling involves managing all aspects of customer contact throughout the relationship in a manner that encourages increased usage, loyalty, and preference for the bank. The cost of customer acquisition and the increased profitability of long-term relationships dictate that customers be won and then kept. Establishment of methodical improvements in service quality and service recovery is a necessary part of building a high-performance sales culture.

One common characteristic of managers in banks that have weak sales cultures is their belief that profitability improvement will be modest and difficult to substantiate in either the short or the long term. Yet the profitability of retail and commercial calling forces varies dramatically among banks in similar markets and of similar size—often a performance difference of 75 to 100 percent. Complacency with average performance is the largest sales culture barrier faced by any management team. A high-performance sales culture yields tangible and readily measurable improvements in profitability and market share, in comparison to peer banks.

Constructing a second-generation sales culture does not necessarily involve spending large sums of money in training,

automation, and incentives. However, building a high-performance sales culture does take both strong management commitment and substantial use of existing internal resources. A properly executed transition should balance the use of resources
among many different concepts, ideas, and improvements.
Building a sales culture is a continuous and ongoing process.
Expenditures must be balanced out for long-term effectiveness.

In building a high-performance sales culture, senior management should establish specific goals. The investment of time and
effort requires a return in terms of improved profitability or
market share. Examples of several specific goals include:

- *Expanding Customer Relationship Depth.* Customers,
  whether wholesale or retail, often have multiple financial
  service company relationships. This fact highlights a key
  opportunity for growth: a bank's existing customer base.
  Customer acquisition costs are a major expense in providing banking services. The cost of acquiring *additional business from existing customers* is far less than the cost of
  acquiring *the same business from new customers.* Identifying customers who have the capability to expand their
  banking relationships, and then selectively offering them
  reasons to increase their relationships, are the keys to relationship depth expansion.

- *Upgrading the Customer Base.* To improve profitability,
  high-performance banks regularly identify and either eliminate or convert unprofitable wholesale and retail customers. The process of redefining the bank's customer base
  depends on being able to determine individual customer relationship profitability. A bank should target 5 to 10 percent
  of its most unprofitable customers yearly and approach
  them for relationship repricing, product use expansion, or
  selective relationship abandonment. Regardless of which
  option is pursued, the bank's profitability will improve.
  Even in the case of selective abandonment, virtually every
  bank is better off reallocating its excess capacity and overhead in the direction of activities that will ultimately earn

healthy returns. A strong sales culture and properly executed approach typically allow a bank to "convert" over 60 percent of these targeted customers into profitable relationships through repricing or relationship expansion.

- *Increasing Spreads, Fees, and Margins.* Building a sales culture *does not* involve lowering margins on a relationship basis to encourage volume, unless the bank is a low-cost provider of certain services and wishes to maximize this advantage. Most banks are not low-cost providers. In a few cases where a market is growing rapidly, trading off short-term profits for market share may at times be the most profitable long-term strategy. However, by cutting prices in mature or marginally growing markets, most banks are playing the precise game that low-cost providers want them to play. Guess who will win in the long term?

- *Enhancing Intercompany Synergy.* Although a basic objective, intercompany synergy is not maximized within most banks. High-performance banks ensure that product knowledge, incentives, participation, and goals exist that lead to a high rate of qualified leads and referrals throughout their corporations.

- *Improving Product and Relationship Profitability.* To improve profitability, a bank must be able to identify and focus on its most profitable market and customer sectors. Unfortunately, traditional sales goals are often based on revenue and other benchmarks that may be indirect and crude measures of profitability. A key management tool used to build a high-performance sales culture is the ability to determine, on a fully loaded basis, profitability by individual products and customer relationships. Calculating earnings per calling officer, branch, or market is a direct extension of this capability. Managers will no longer have to guess which customers are most profitable and should be given appropriate attention. The most profitable market segments can be identified, and business development efforts can be concentrated. Unprofitable products or relationships can be identified, altered, or discontinued.

Profitable products can be accurately identified and then enhanced or promoted with increased effort. Fee-based products can be priced at a profit. The importance of accurate assessment of product and customer profitability is the foundation of a high-performance sales culture.

- *Increasing Share of Target Markets.* This is a self-explanatory and perpetual management goal.

The challenges faced in trying to reach and sustain these goals are formidable. Increased competition, customer sophistication, overcapacity, and price sensitivity are obstacles that will disable and batter most banks into submission—and disappointing results. The ability to build a high-performance sales culture, which will overcome these obstacles through increased value-added and sales effectiveness, will be an attribute of the winners.

This book addresses a methodical eight-point program for building a high-performance sales culture. Each point consists of a collection of ideas that can be implemented with proven results to provide a competitive edge:

1. *Providing Effective Sales Management.* Top ideas for improving and formalizing sales management, modifying performance appraisals, and converting to more accurate measurement tools are discussed in Chapter 2.

2. *Streamlining the Organization for Higher Sales Effectiveness.* Proven strategies (such as tiering key positions, creating advanced organizational structures, and redefining sales positions) are covered in Chapter 3.

3. *Staffing Employees Who Have Sales Aptitudes.* Strategies such as sales test screening, interview profile improvements, initial pay strategies, top performer retention, and handling of nonperformers are examined in Chapter 4.

4. *Providing Effective Sales Training.* Concepts such as sales certification, advanced referral training, enhancement of sales curricula, improvement of product training, and negotiations with sales training vendors are discussed in Chapter 5.

5. *Equipping Employees with Functional Sales Aids and Tools.* Sales tracking and business development tools, which are badly needed by front-line personnel if they are to perform well, are a few of the ideas that are covered in Chapter 6.

6. *Improving Corporate Communications and Referrals.* The building of competitive intelligence, sales recognition, referral, and customer feedback information exchange systems is critical to sales culture success. This process is addressed in Chapter 7.

7. *Instituting Effective Rewards and Incentives.* Increasing employees' effectiveness and capacity to bring in new business through both nonmonetary and incentive-based rewards is reviewed in detail throughout Chapters 8 and 9.

8. *Improving Service and Retaining Existing Customers.* Customer retention value, defection analysis, service recovery systems, and quality service circles are a few ideas used by banks with high-performance sales cultures. They are covered in Chapter 10.

Every bank that strives for a second-generation sales culture must ultimately assemble its own plan of action. In the long term, only those firms that (1) can build and maintain a sales culture, (2) are evolutionary and adaptable to their specific markets, and (3) provide excellence in value added and innovation, will be able to grow in market share and provide consistently high earnings.

2

Organizational Enhancement

Most banks with high-performance sales cultures have dedicated sales positions in each area whose primary or sole responsibility is business development and the creation of revenue. For decades, leading banks have enjoyed great success with dedicated sales positions (originally on the wholesale side and then expanded to the retail side) that concentrate solely on new business development, cold calling, and prospecting. Once the prospective customer is qualified or the sale is closed, the customer is frequently turned over to a relationship banker who provides account servicing and is highly trained in cross-selling additional products. Sales-officer compensation packages usually contain a high proportion of incentives closely tied to relationship profitability. Because sales officers are chosen for their business development skills and engage in selling and prospecting on a full-time basis, their penetration and closing skills are generally far more effective than those of normal relationship managers, who have multiple responsibilities. The meticulous separation of operational and sales duties in both wholesale and retail areas—without creating functional or reporting duplicity, which weighs down performance—is critical in the creation of a high-performance sales culture.

A major hurdle that every bank faces when implementing dedicated sales-officer positions is the reluctance of relationship managers to give up their top prospects. Management must insist that a prospect is of little value to a bank—only customers are. To ensure the success of sales positions and to maximize bank revenue, senior management must insist that most strong prospects be handed over to the sales officers.

Dedicated sales managers typically have direct responsibility over sales officers. Although a strong working knowledge of banking is helpful, many banks have reported great success in hiring experienced sales managers from other industries. An outsider is especially valuable when chosen to be the senior sales manager and to lead the overall sales effort. Because that individual is already a capable and proven sales manager, both the learning curve and chances of failure are greatly reduced, compared with those of an internal manager with no sales management experience. The full backing and support of senior management are critical to the success of the senior sales manager.

Organizational structure not only affects the sales capability of individual departments, it also influences the level of cross-selling, referrals, and synergy that a bank will be able to generate. The organizational changes described in this chapter have been critical to the sales success of leading banks.

❑ HYBRID RETAIL AND SMALL-BUSINESS CALLING FORCE

In banks where the retail side is also responsible for small-business development, a hybrid system of split responsibility between branch managers and dedicated calling officers usually creates the most effective calling force. In such a hybrid system, dedicated calling officers are responsible for small-business development by specialized industry in regions of high business density. In more remote areas, small-business concentrations are located, the most central branches are identified, and the bank's top branch managers are reassigned to these centralized branches. The branch managers are then given additional product knowledge and commercial credit training, and the branches operate as regional small-business banking and sales centers. Such hybrid systems share considerable advantages over retail divisions which assign small-business development responsibilities to all branch managers. The product knowledge needed to sell both credit and noncredit services, combined with multiple-call sales cycles and the need to educate less knowledgeable customers, usually make conventional retail calling systems perform at only average levels.

❏ ORGANIZATIONAL FLATTENING BY REDEFINING MANAGEMENT ROLES

Once relationship managers reach their most productive levels, often after years of training and experience, they are typically placed in line or midlevel management positions. There, most of the new-business development skills and the relationships with customers they have developed and nurtured with customers are wasted. Even the best ability to recruit and train high-caliber relationship managers cannot match the experience and credibility that experienced line and midlevel managers can offer at a business-development meeting with a customer. A bank's best resource for new-business development and retentive selling clearly lies in its line and midlevel managers.

By flattening organizational structures and increasing senior relationship manager and midlevel manager contact with customers, a number of banks have reclaimed this invaluable resource. Redefining management positions entails dedicating a greater percentage of each respective officer's efforts to customer contact and new-business development. Through relationship management teams or direct account assignment, a number of banks have increased their managers' production and revenue-generation capacity.

❏ TIERING SALES POSITIONS

One tactic used frequently by high-performance banks is greatly expanding the number of tiers within each sales position. These banks often have as many as six to eight different tiers for a single position. Relationship managers rise through these tiers based on their sales results, product knowledge, and overall performance merit. Although there is seldom a large pay difference between each tier, great prestige, recognition, and nonmonetary incentives are often attached to each advancement. This technique has been used with considerable success within both the wholesale and retail sides. Progression to each new level leads to a new title. Because the tiers lead to a feeling of quick progression through the bank, they motivate most employees. Upon moving into each new tier, employees are often rewarded with additional training. This has the dual effect of creating job satisfaction and increasing job skills and competency. One bank's experience follows:

> In our retail area, we decided to separate our platform representative positions into six tiers. The tiered titles consist of Platform Representative I–IV, Senior Platform Representative, then Personal Banker. Each subsequent position is earned by sales performance, time in grade, and product knowledge respectively. In addition to slight increases in base salaries, each incremental position also earns a slightly higher incentive commission rate. When the employees reach the level of Personal Banker, they are given a portfolio of our most profitable retail customers and are expected to both provide outstanding personal service and to increase the relationship profitability of these customers. The tiers have been very successful in boosting sales performance and have also lessened turnover rates slightly since promotions to higher tiers are frequent. After our success in the retail area, we decided to expand the tiering system to encompass all line officer positions bank-wide and met with equal success.

Banks have traditionally used positions in small-business or middle-market lending as training areas for their employees, before moving them to the large corporate banking area. Although it is natural to start employees with lesser responsibilities and then gradually move them up, the bank's customers pay a high price in terms of constantly changing relationship managers. Tiering allows management to convert high-turnover areas into areas of long-term commitment while still offering advancement through incremental promotions and career paths.

Certification is frequently used in conjunction with tiering positions. Each employee must demonstrate a certain proficiency in sales and product knowledge before being promoted to a new level. A few banks have even experimented with allowing only the top several tiers to earn incentive pay or referral bonuses. Although one questions whether this demoralizes the lower ranks, in some cases it has decreased turnover, especially for experienced, higher-productivity employees.

❏ REDEPLOYING KEY ACCOUNT MANAGERS

Several top-performing wholesale banking units credit large gains to the redeployment of key national account managers away from large corporate areas. In these banks, key account managers are assigned to the most profitable 10 to 25 percent of existing business customers. They are completely responsible for relationship profitability and for the expansion of business with key customers. Key account managers are typically selected from the very best of a bank's relationship managers and business-development specialists. They receive training in relationship profitability criteria and meet with key customers regularly, to tune prices and products used, and to introduce and sell new products in order to maximize profitability. A total focus on maintaining or achieving the lead-bank relationship is critical. These relationship managers are often permanently assigned to the accounts, providing great stability with the bank's key customers.

❏ BUILDING AN ADVANCED ORGANIZATIONAL STRUCTURE

A basic market-oriented organizational structure is illustrated in the top half of Figure 2–1 on the following page. All relationship managers, whether branch managers, commercial calling officers, or trust calling officers, are housed within specific departments. Because of this, commercial calling officers are often isolated from the institutional trust area, unless these calling officers are on a joint call, are visiting with a specialist,

BASIC MARKET-ORIENTED STRUCTURE

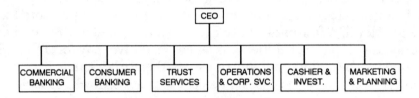

PROTOTYPE MARKET-ORIENTED STRUCTURE

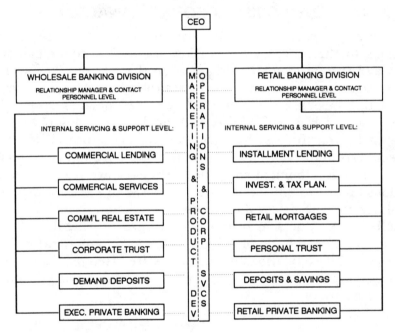

Figure 2-1 Organizational Structures

or are being artifically rewarded through incentives. Similarly, branch managers often do not feel comfortable representing the bank's investment, private banking, or personal trust areas. Although rewarding employees for referrals is a partial solution, substantial business opportunities are lost because of this traditional organizational structure.

In addition, marketing support on the wholesale side is often weak, because the marketing area is usually more comfortable with retail products and does not report to the wholesale area. Product development is a long, drawn-out process because of the separation among product managers in marketing, line areas, and operations. The most elaborate interdepartmental committee meetings and senior management guidance will still not deliver the new and differentiated products demanded by customers in a competitive timeframe. Furthermore, each department is more interested in the margins earned from its own products and services than in increased profitability from raising customer-relationship margins across multiple departments. These cumulative shortcomings suggest the need for a more efficient market-oriented structure.

Consider the prototype market-oriented structure presented in the bottom diagram in Figure 2–1. The primary difference between this model and the first one is that most relationship managers and customer-contact personnel are housed under either wholesale or retail banking areas instead of under specialized departments, several of which may serve the same target markets. These relationship managers are expected to represent all bank services in the target markets that they serve.

Senior managers in both the wholesale and retail areas now have the ability to focus relationship managers on customer-relationship profitability instead of on departmental products. Management may still assign relationship managers to specialized areas (i.e. private banking, asset-based lending, etc.) but the officers would still directly represent other areas (i.e. private banking specialists would directly represent personal trust, investments, estate planning, brokerage, small-business lending, etc.). Where before it took substantial cooperation between multiple employees, departments, policies, and a great deal of luck, one relationship manager can now provide a total answer to the customer's needs.

With this prototype organizational structure, relationship managers are supported by servicing specialists who focus exclusively on their areas. Marketing is involved at all levels, from market strategy and planning at the senior level to direct support of line officers in every department. To reduce overhead, marketing specialists, who are often one and the same as the product managers, work with each department in designing and promoting products. Forcing broad integration of marketing and operations management leads to a thorough understanding of each other's capabilities and needs. This increase in understanding and communication yields better and more reliable products, precisely when they are desired by the market.

Relationship managers remain focused on and are rewarded for total relationship profitability. Cross-departmental territory disputes are virtually eliminated. Each relationship manager is able to address *all* of a targeted customer's needs and to provide an innovative and differentiated service. Sales call costs are reduced because calls by multiple officers from various departments are eliminated—an advantage to customers as well.

Although no specific organizational structure is best for all banks, prototype and hybrid organizational structures offer a primary opportunity for improvements that will better meet customer needs and changing environments.

❏ FORMALIZING CAREER ADVANCEMENT THROUGH SALES

A fundamental step in most high-performance sales cultures is the posturing of performance in sales and sales management as a major determinant in career advancement. Changes often include modifying positions to retain and promote good sales performers, adjusting performance appraisals to heavily weight sales accomplishment, and restructuring traditional career tracks to include both sales and sales management. Career advancement through sales performance sends a clear and convincing message throughout the organization, regarding the importance of sales achievement.

❏ SALES AND SALES MANAGEMENT CAREER TRACKS

In structuring career paths, it is important to tailor advancement to coincide with the sales performer's own values and ambitions. Because of a higher motivation for monetary reward, top sales performers sometimes prefer to retain existing positions rather than to enter management, especially when incentive plans are aggressive and there is a greater potential to earn higher pay by staying in a line sales position. It is important, then, to establish two alternative career paths for top sales performers. One path should allow top performers to advance through line sales positions that increase in importance, pay, and grade. The other path should include escalating sales management positions.

On the retail side, an example of continual advancement of platform representatives through line positions was discussed earlier. The management track might include advancement into a position as branch sales manager. This position would provide branch managers with needed sales management assistance over the platform representatives, but would also include traditional platform responsibilities. The next step might be a position as regional platform sales manager, in charge of platform sales in multiple branches, etc. Line advancement for branch managers might include small-business relationship management. The sales management path might include a redefined district-branch management position, attainable through successful branch sales management.

Similar dual tracks should be formalized in each major wholesale area. Understanding of career paths in sales and sales management is critical to the long-term performance of any sales culture.

❏ FORMALIZING SALES LEADERSHIP

A number of banks have established a *sales leadership committee* that ensures a high-performance sales culture. This committee usually consists of the chief executive officer (CEO) or other top officers, the marketing director, department heads or highly market-drive officers from each department, and selected senior officers who have demonstrated beneficial leadership roles. The committee serves to provide sales leadership, visibility, and execution throughout the bank. It is often assisted by *sales advisory committees* representing each department or area. Each sales advisory committee consists of one member of the sales leadership committee and the most market-driven officers within each department or area. Each committee meets regularly and discusses ways to increase sales performance and to lower customer-defection rates, in order to improve profitability in its specific area. The sales advisory committees then submit recommendations and ideas to the sales leadership committee on a regular basis, and they also serve as sounding boards for strategies and changes.

❏ MODIFYING LENDING-AUTHORITY CENTRALIZATION

The saying that most banks break themselves during good economic times, rather than bad, is still true today. Senior management often decentralizes and increases officer lending authority during periods of strong economic growth, in order to be responsive to customers and remain competitive with other banks. When economic growth inevitably slows, inconsistent portfolios become unprofitable, the misdirected sales culture comes to a sudden halt, and the credit policy area predictably recentralizes lending authority to impose better control of credit standards.

To eliminate the temptation to decentralize credit and lending authority during good economic times, it is vital that credit administration have a turnaround time equal or superior to the bank's competitors. Loans channeled to loan committees must meet these same high turnaround standards, often necessitating more frequent but shorter loan committee meetings. Superior credit-administration turnaround ensures a lasting competitive advantage in both good economic times and bad. Centralized lending authority with exceptional turnaround time eliminates the need to decentralize lending authority, ensures consistent portfolios, and is critical to the long-term development and survival of a high-performance sales culture.

Lending-authority centralization allows relationship managers to focus more time on business development and sales, and to participate heavily in incentive plans. The reduction of individual and chain sign-off authority also reduces the potential for acceptance of marginal loans to meet volume incentives. Incentive participation at all levels is essential to the development of a strong sales culture.

☐ CRITERIA FOR SEPARATION OF SALES AND OPERATIONAL DUTIES

On the wholesale side, the division of operational and sales duties usually falls into one of two philosophies. Customer surveys often indicate that business and other wholesale clients prefer to deal with bank officers who have direct authority to approve loans or are strong influencers in the approval process, and who are able to make various other commitments on behalf of the bank. Banks subscribing to this philosophy believe they can differentiate their banking services by staffing positions with officers who perform a wide range of duties, with sales only one part of the total. These banks improve performance by increased sales support, which allows relationship managers to focus more time and effort on business development. Lower-overhead employees can often take care of many operational, administrative, and correspondence duties typically performed by these relationship managers. This strategy has been most successful in positions needing considerable sophistication and expertise, such as corporate finance and underwriting; most investment banks are structured in this manner. Senior managers and officers in these banks have both considerable authority and direct calling responsibilities.

Other banks subscribe to a different philosophy. Because most significant credit approval is done by committee or chain sign-off, there is little advantage in having a relationship manager with operational, credit, *and* sales responsibilities. Such banks realize greater success by having dedicated sales officers involved solely in business development. By historically evaluating their relationship managers based on their business development success, they have been able to assemble a team of highly effective sales officers. Candidates hired from the outside often have previous sales experience and are expected to perform well in their sales positions. The superior prospecting, relationship management, and closing skills of dedicated sales officers provide these banks with a strong competitive advantage over competing banks, in relatively less sophisticated areas such as middle-market and small-business calling.

To maximize calling effectiveness, it is possible to use both strategies. High-performance banks apply the appropriate strategy, depending on the individual characteristics and sophistication demanded by each market.

❏ REARRANGING PROFIT CENTERS

Traditionally, department managers have had few rewards for engaging in teamwork across multiple departments, providing interdepartmental relationship pricing, encouraging referrals, or increasing calling-force efficiency. In some instances, departments have actually been penalized for offering relationship pricing to expand relationships, because lower revenue per product appears to lower the profitability of individual departments (despite higher overall bank profitability).

To counteract the appearance of lower margins during relationship pricing, a number of banks have grouped *all* of their relationship managers into the same profit center. Profit-center consolidation on the wholesale side often includes commercial lending, asset-based lending, institutional trust, and real estate lending. A few banks have implemented the same strategy on the retail side, by skillfully rearranging the profit centers of the retail, private banking, and individual trust areas, in order to encourage cooperation. Group profitability incentives further encourage cooperation among department heads and their relationship managers.

❏ BUILDING RELATIONSHIP MANAGEMENT TEAMS

In creating *relationship management teams*, two or three bankers work together as part of a larger group. The senior banker devotes most of his or her time to business development and calling efforts. The junior officer primarily performs administrative duties, documentation, follow-up details, credit work (where applicable), and a limited amount of business development. This achieves several objectives:

- The division of duties allows the more experienced officers, or those officers who have the best sales and calling skills, to focus on sales, new business development, and fee-income generation.
- A chief complaint among wholesale customers, relationship manager turnover, is sharply reduced: Junior officers know their customers and become ready successors.
- Customer service and accessibility are improved because at least two officers are familiar with and work on every account.
- The most experienced and knowledgeable officers are the customer's primary contact—the "best foot forward" principle.
- The junior officer has time to learn sales skills and become familiar with the products, while still being immediately productive for the bank.
- Selling is perceived as a privileged activity reserved for only the most knowledgeable officers.

❑ BRANCH REDEPLOYMENT

In many high-performance banks, top retail management takes full advantage of specialized retail branch strategies. In some cases, 25 to 30 percent of all branches are targeted as senior-citizen branches, miniature-deposit branches, nontraditional investment branches, university branches, transaction branches, or upscale and affluent branches, and are given specialized marketing layouts. The design, staffing, and size of each office are directly related to maximizing the profitability of serving a defined market. Table 2–1 highlights common specialty branches.

Table 2–1 Common Retail Specialty Branches

	Senior Citizen Deposit Branches
Strategy	Collect high deposits with minimal overhead and prepackaged products.
Logistics	Small area of under 600 sq. ft. (64 sq. m.) located in and around retirement centers, retirement villages, large nursing homes, and other locations of high convenience to senior citizens. Personnel requirements include one platform representative who doubles as a P/R teller and one additional representative in higher-volume branches or during peak periods (some banks even hire from the local senior citizen labor pool).
	Affluent or Upscale Branches
Strategy	High-volume cross-sell of *all* bank services (including nontraditional) and collection of high deposits.
Logistics	Highly automated facility with a comfortable, staffed reception area. Exclusive sit-down service delivered completely by top-performing relationship managers in enclosed, well-appointed offices (no tellers) with convenient hours and appointments.
	Investment Branches
Strategy	Accumulate deposits and earn fee income by offering deposit and nontraditional investment products through a tiny, minimally staffed storefront facility in upscale downtown and highly affluent areas.
Logistics	Minimally staffed by highly skilled "investment counselors" offering a full range of products. No cash handling or traditional transactions with the exception of deposits and purchases of nontraditional investment

Table 2–1 (*continued*)

products. Clear signage to eliminate transactional walk-ins and to encourage deposits and investments.

University Branches

Strategy   Accumulate deposits and maximize relationship profitability by minimizing overhead and servicing costs.

Logistics   Small, minimally staffed new account opening facility equipped with ATMs to handle virtually all customer transactions. Other ATMs positioned strategically at various parts of the university campus to handle transaction volume, provide easy access, and earn fee income from noncustomer transactions.

Full-Service Senior Citizen Branches

Strategy   Attract a large share of the market and accumulate above-average deposits in areas or vicinities with a large percentage of retirees and other senior citizens.

Logistics   Comfortable, senior-citizen-specific branches with ease of entry and exit, hand rails, larger parking spots, large signage, relaxed waiting area, functional senior furniture, and special services to differentiate the bank (coffee service, television in waiting area, etc.). Senior prepackaged products are extremely popular.

Source: Council on Financial Competition. *Retail Excellence II Aggressive Branch Sales* Washington, DC: The Advisory Board, 1987, pp. 114–117.

❏ TASK FORCE TO REDUCE SALES BARRIERS

One of the first steps that senior management should take is to organize a task force to identify sales barriers and make recommendations to reduce them. By examining daily workloads and tasks performed by all employees who have sales or sales management responsibility, this task force can identify areas where work can be streamlined. Eliminating or merging required reports and forms, reducing redundant or unnecessary procedures or roles, automating repetitive or burdensome tasks, and reassigning some tasks to nonsales personnel are typical recommendations.

❏ PARALLEL RETAIL SALES STRUCTURE

On the retail side, implementing parallel sales and sales management positions next to operational positions has always been controversial because of the often confusing reporting structure and additional personnel overhead that result. However, several top-performing banks have been extremely successful in instituting parallel structures in high-volume branches that primarily serve upscale customers. In these branches, incremental gains in both revenues and margins more than offset increased overhead.

Once appropriate branches are selected, sales managers are hired or internally designated and then placed in charge of two to five branches each. Sales positions within each branch are further isolated from operational responsibilities and transformed into fully dedicated sales positions reporting directly to a sales manager instead of to the operational branch manager. A senior retail sales manager position, with overall responsibility for sales results in the selected branches, should also be created. The advantages of establishing a parallel retail sales structure include the rapid transformation of the selected branches into sales-driven units, better sales management support of individual efforts, and the ability to staff newly created positions with candidates who have proven sales skills and backgrounds.

❑ SALES SUPPORT MANAGERS

In addition to sales managers, another method of assisting the sales effort is by assigning select officers to the position of *sales support manager*. Duties and responsibilities include:

- Providing managers with partial agendas, training aids, product profiles, and ideas they can use during sales meetings. Partial agendas ensure consistency in sales training throughout the bank and provide managers with specific topics of responsibility, to be covered during sales meetings.
- Coaching individual relationship managers, branch managers, and sales managers on a regular basis.
- Providing follow-up on participants' goals and progress after sales training.
- Participating in and assisting with sales meetings bankwide.
- Providing feedback and sales suggestions to managers and trainers.

The impact on the overall sales culture makes the creation of these rotational positions well worth exploring. The promotion to sales support manager can be used as an intermediary step before individuals are promoted to midlevel and senior management positions. It is imperative that the individual chosen to be sales support manager be a respected top performer in the area of business development and sales.

❑ CUSTOMER ADVOCATES

A number of high-performance banks have established *customer advocates* within all departments. Customer advocate responsibilities, which are often added to an existing position, entail being the customers' champion. By being present during all relevant meetings, customer advocates speak out when policies, procedures, or other actions would reduce the level of utility or service for the bank's customers. Customer advocates serve as useful reminders that most bank decisions directly affect its present and prospective customers.

❏ PLATFORM SALES COORDINATORS

Several banks have added *platform sales coordinators* to their retail systems. These individuals, often top veteran platform representatives, are in essence platform sales managers. The actual structure of this position varies. In some banks, the top platform representative within each branch becomes the platform sales coordinator, reporting to the branch manager. In a few banks, a single platform sales coordinator reporting to the head of branch administration assists in the sales support and the organization of platform sales meetings, bankwide. This position is sometimes an intermediary step for banks that allow their top platform representatives to become assistant branch managers. The experience of one bank follows:

Although our branch managers have traditionally held the responsibility of providing sales management support to our platform representatives, we decided that we needed to substantially increase sales support and promoted our very best platform representatives with leadership qualities to the new position of platform sales coordinator. Although pay increases are modest, we make a substantial investment in terms of training in sales coaching and product knowledge to ensure that these platform sales coordinators will be well equipped for their new positions. Once they return to their three assigned branches, they are expected to work with each and every platform representative, provide sales coaching on a daily basis, and assist customers during heavy traffic periods when overflow develops. In addition, our platform sales coordinators are also in charge of product knowledge training at the line level, new product launches, and experience sharing among all platform representatives. They are evaluated based on platform sales improvement in the branches which they support.

❏ FLOATING FIELD SALES TRAINERS

A highly successful innovation has been the designation of *floating field sales trainers*. These positions are often staffed by top-performing relationship managers, officers, platform representatives, or even sales training professionals who float among various field locations, providing sales coaching on a full- or part-time basis. Such individuals will usually spend 1 to 5 days in each area, department, or branch, on a rotational basis, and will work individually with each relationship manager, officer, or platform representative. Direct coaching and training have dramatically increased sales performance in many banks.

On the retail side, floating field sales trainers are often equivalent to platform sales coordinators (described earlier). On the commercial side, highly trained sales-training specialists or top-performing relationship managers make joint calls and provide sales coaching, to augment the department/area manager's role. In several banks, before being promoted to management, top relationship managers perform this floating sales training function in addition to their regular duties.

❏ PLATFORM LENDING ASSISTANTS

A number of banks have trained and enabled their top branch platform representatives to take loan applications, handle loan documentation, and provide funds disbursement. The objectives include:

- Freeing loan officers' time, to allow them to focus on increased new-business development and in-branch sales management
- Decreasing the loan customer's waiting time during peak periods
- Providing job advancement and progressive duties for top platform representatives

- Providing top platform representatives with experience before becoming loan officers

Once the platform representatives have taken the loan application, it passes to branch loan officers or to the centralized processing center for approval. The *platform lending assistant* then handles disbursement and documentation. Although additional training is necessary, such programs have been generally well received by the branch officers, as long as they receive credit for the loans.

❑ ACCOUNT CLOSING SPECIALISTS

A number of banks have successfully trained and established an elite corps that specializes in dealing with account closing requests. These *account closing specialists* are often domiciled within each department on the wholesale side or in centralized phone centers on the retail side. When a customer asks to close an account, the relationship manager or platform representative attempts to persuade the customer to maintain the account, if in good status. If the relationship manager is unsuccessful at persuading the customer to retain the account, the customer is then *immediately* connected to an account closing specialist who will close regardless of the reason.

The highly trained account closing specialists are empowered with an arsenal of service recovery tools for such matters as crediting accounts directly, sending flowers to estranged customers, or providing remote mail banking kits. They have the authority to immediately implement actions and decisions that may lead to recovering the account. The account closing specialists are typically given incentives for their performance in customer recovery. These incentives are often delayed up to one month, to ensure that a recovery was both implemented and effective. It is vital that normal relationship managers be trained in service recovery and expected to first attempt to retain the customer, before passing the customer to the account closing specialists.

Centralized account closing has the added benefit of facilitating immediate and consistent feedback to senior management.

The account closing specialists are trained to identify all aspects of the bank's services that did not meet the customer's expectations and to relay this information to management. Several banks have taken this a step further, as the following example illustrates:

> In order to be more attuned to customer needs and as part of our sales and service quality program, all senior officers are expected to monitor our centralized account closing lines at least one hour per week. In addition, several of the officers have taken it upon themselves to actually answer the lines and speak to the customers directly. It has been amazing to watch how quickly chronic operational and service problems have been corrected. Centralized account closing has breathed new life into our customer retention and satisfaction programs.

❑ RELATIONSHIP RECOVERY SPECIALISTS

Customers who leave because of dissatisfaction subject a bank to tremendous costs. These costs include replacement expense in the form of new customer acquisition, lost future business from the alienated customer, and lost future business from potential prospects because of ill will. If a bank is to maximize growth and reduce its opportunity costs, a substantial number of these customers must be won back and then kept.

To accomplish the goal of winning back alienated customers on the retail side, specially trained teams of *relationship recovery specialists* should regularly make contact with lost customers and attempt to rebuild the relationship. Like account closing specialists, these employees must have an arsenal of recovery tools available and the authority to take immediate and responsible steps to win back customers. Banks that have properly implemented both account closing and relationship recovery teams are often surprised at their effectiveness and rapid payback.

❑ PERSONAL BANKERS FOR HIGH-VALUE CUSTOMERS

The banks that have been most successful at building high-value customer (HVC) loyalty are those that have surveyed all targeted customers first, to determine whether they would like highly personalized service. On the basis of this survey, the bank follows up with customers who desire personalized service, and these customers are assigned, or choose, personal bankers who are highly experienced and proven platform representatives. Each personal banker serves as the HVC's primary contact and, over time, builds a solid relationship. The survey process also identifies those customers who would misuse the service, simply wanting the fastest attention possible from the first available representative, and who place little value on having a personal banker relationship. The survey results also allow relationship managers and personal bankers to concentrate their efforts on high-value customers who desire a personal banker relationship.

❏ MODIFYING ADMINISTRATIVE ASSISTANT ROLES

Account service duties such as documentation, correspondence, proposals, reports, and problem-solving tasks consume a large percentage of a relationship manager's available business-development time. Top banks frequently examine and identify nonrevenue-generating tasks handled by both wholesale and retail relationship managers. Wherever appropriate, some tasks are switched to administrative assistants, who are given additional training. Modifying administrative assistant positions substantially increases business development and sales time for each relationship manager.

❏ MODIFYING THE TRAINING REPORTING STRUCTURE

Sales training is typically structured as a human resources function reporting to the Director of Human Resources. Many banks have deviated from this course with great success, often having sales trainers report directly to branch administration on the retail side and to corporate banking on the wholesale side.

The purpose of this organizational change is twofold. First, it provides a more direct link between trainers and the line, which increases accountability and support. Second, it provides trainers with more opportunities, after training delivery, to supply continuous follow-up and coaching to the line. Follow-up is crucial to building a sales culture and, when properly executed, often plays a greater role in skills internalization than the training itself. Most successful organizational structures that centralize training under Human Resources have strong dotted-line responsibilities to the supported department.

Top-performing banks often emphasize the importance of sales training by regularly assigning a top midlevel officer to an 18- to 24-month rotation as the head of sales training. Critical to the success of this assignment is a substantial promotion immediately after completion of the rotation. The results are that the selection or promotion of top performers for the job emphasizes the career opportunities open to them and identifies sales performance as an important measure of achievement.

3

Advanced Sales Management

Consistent and exceptional sales management is critical to the success of a high-performance sales culture. Even if a bank provides sales management training and encourages sales meetings, too many factors are left to chance. Although some managers will perform well, just as many will perform below expectation. The following concepts have helped achieve *consistent* sales management teams in a number of leading banks.

❏ RESTRUCTURING TRADITIONAL SALES MEETING FORMATS

A key to providing effective sales support is the *sales management meeting*, at which managers establish the itinerary for upcoming department and branch sales meetings. This monthly meeting, which is usually held one week prior to scheduled sales meetings, is best kept as a completely independent adjunct to other management meetings. It allows management at all levels to discuss mutual problems and solutions and ensures unified sales management efforts, goals, and strategies throughout the bank. Most important, it is a planning meeting.

Sales meeting planning tools such as itineraries, handouts, role-play cases, and interdepartmental speaker arrangements are established during the meeting. The sales management meeting eliminates planning duplicity or failure in the field by time-constrained managers and ensures a uniform sales culture throughout the various departments and branches.

Other vital functions of the sales management meeting are: to share prospects and leads with various departments, to eliminate service and turf conflicts over customers who use multiple departments, and to establish avenues and strategies for joint calling and teamwork among all bank areas. The more bonding and networking that takes place in each meeting, the better the attitudes and effectiveness of all sales managers. These sessions should preferably be headed by senior management, in order to reinforce both support and commitment for the sales culture. Table 3–1 lists topics commonly covered during bankwide sales management meetings.

To be effective, mandatory department or branch *sales meetings* should be held at least once a month. The sales meetings should be supplemented with daily sales assemblies. Because many department and branch managers are not natural sales managers, it is crucial that the itinerary of each sales meeting be established at the monthly sales management meeting.

An itinerary should be prepared for the sales meeting and distributed to the participants at least one day in advance. These meetings should include role playing to internalize any skills or product knowledge learned. In addition to group discussions, managers should consider dividing the group into teams of two or three individuals. Each of these teams can discuss a tactic/product approach, quickly practice a role play and perform before the entire group for feedback and discussion. Managers frequently create sales meeting competitions and reward winners. Highly effective breakouts can be done in as little as 15 to 20 minutes. Rotating the participants in each team is important. Topics commonly covered in department or branch sales meetings are also listed in Table 3–1.

A number of banks effectively use daily department or branch *sales assemblies* lasting between 10 and 15 minutes. During each assembly, the manager quickly reviews the business and revenue results of the previous day and establishes

Table 3-1   Sales Meeting Topics

Sales Management Meeting Topics **Frequency: Monthly (two weeks prior to sales meetings).**	
Senior management review of performance.	Planning of upcoming sales meetings.
Discussions of mutual problems and solutions.	Organizing interdepartmental product briefings.
Briefing on upcoming contest incentives.	Organizing interdepartmental joint calling.
Briefing on upcoming promotions and advertising.	Sharing of referrals and prospects.
Briefing on product changes or enhancements.	Presentation of sales management awards.
Sales management success and tips (roundtable).	Distribution of sales management incentives.
Setting of sales goals and strategy.	Sales culture encouragement by senior management.

Sales Meeting Topics **Frequency: Monthly or biweekly.**	
Management update on past sales performance.	Tips on selling against the competition.
Product knowledge training and role playing.	Group feedback on all role playing.
Briefing on product changes and enhancements.	Product knowledge briefings from other areas.

Table 3–1 (*continued*)

Service quality training.	Suggestions for next sales meeting.
Sales skills training and role playing.	Briefing on upcoming contest incentives.
Handling objections or complaints.	Briefing on upcoming promotionals and advertising.
Effective referral training and role playing.	Presentation of sales awards.
Sales success and tips (roundtable).	Distribution of sales incentives.

Sales Assembly Topics
Frequency: Daily.

Review of previous day's customer and revenue results.	Tips on selling against the competition.
Setting of individual goals for the day ahead.	Sales success and tips (roundtable).
Individual coaching after the assembly.	Recognition of previous day's top performers.

individual goals and strategies for the day ahead. As a daily routine, sales assemblies ensure that, each day, every relationship manager or customer contact person has an established sales goal and business purpose. Table 3–1 lists common topics covered during a sales assembly.

The meetings described above should never be cancelled. If they are, the employees will sense that the task of building a sales team is not a top priority and the sales culture will be severely undermined. A manager must expect a high level of attendance and participation from each of the employees. Sales meetings should be mandatory. This requirement can be reinforced by paying out monthly incentive only at the meetings or by using door prizes, auctions, and raffles.

❏ BUILDING A COMPETITIVE ENVIRONMENT

One of a bank's worst enemies in its marketplace is a lack of visibly threatening competitors. The actions and tactics of one bank might affect another's profitability in only subtle ways, but, without visual confrontation, a bank often has trouble molding itself into a "team" to outperform or outsell competitors.

By creating strong internal competition among divisions, departments, and branches, senior management can increase overall profitability and sales volume. Teams can be organized to compete on call volume, sales volume, profitability, and so on, and handicaps can be established between departments and the results posted weekly. Team captains should be trained to motivate their team members. Here is one bank's experience on the retail side:

> We encourage high performance by holding bankwide competitions every week. Platform representatives in each branch compete on performance figures that they directly influence (handicapped and expressed as a percentage of historical data to ensure fair competition between branches of different volumes). Branch managers compete weekly on performance figures for variables that they directly influence. Our regional managers compete against each other based on total regional performance. Since

performance is expressed as a percentage of the increase in volume or profit in relation to previous years, our retail branches can also directly compete against the trust department, commercial loan area, and other units. Contests are run on a quarterly basis and are ongoing. We credit this system with creating a highly visible and tangible competitive atmosphere throughout our bank, which encourages exceptional performance and profitability.

Another technique to improve performance is a focus on one or two specific competitors. This creates a sense of purpose, teamwork, and urgency. Competitive information is distributed to the field frequently, as it becomes available. In this manner, some banks have established highly visible competitors and then plotted strategies to outperform the opponent in profitability, market share, and similar measures.

Rewards can be either in intangibles, or in incentive payouts, depending on senior management's philosophy. Both incentives and nonfinancial rewards are discussed extensively in the following chapters. Although developing visible competition requires the establishment of competitive criteria and their administration, it is highly effective in generating the competitive atmosphere that is necessary for a high-performance sales culture.

❏ CREATING HEROES

If management is willing and able to create heroes among top sales performers, a strong separation of high-performance sales cultures from average performers results. "What gets rewarded gets repeated." This adage is especially appropriate in creating a top sales culture. By elevating the bank's top revenue producers to "hero" status, management sends a clear signal to all other employees about its value system and what it recognizes as good performance.

❏ DISTRIBUTING GOALS TO THE LINE

When bankwide sales goals are established, these goals are usually divided among relevant department and branch managers;

each becomes accountable for a certain amount of revenue and profits. Unfortunately, this is where the process usually ends. Goals are seldom subdivided and assigned to each line employee. Line officers and customer contact employees are often not aware of the revenues they must individually generate, in order to pull their weight. Instead, they are asked to meet such vague targets as cross-sell ratios on the retail side, or loan volume and quality standards on the commercial side. Although the importance of such items is unquestionable, each employee and the employee's manager should be informed of the exact revenue and profit levels they need to produce.

❏ JOINT SETTING OF INDIVIDUAL GOALS

One of the most important roles of the sales manager is to set goals jointly in one-on-one meetings with each sales employee. It is vital that the employee be a part of the decision-making process. By involving each employee, the manager can ensure that all employees establish ownership of the goals set. If this buy-in is accomplished successfully, there is a much greater chance that employees will meet and even surpass the goals agreed on. The goals set should be specific, measurable, achievable, and challenging. The basic process is as follows:

1. The sales manager should meet with the employees as a group, to explain the importance of establishing individual goals, how the goals will affect the employees, and the joint process by which the manager will follow up with each employee.

2. The sales manager then holds one-on-one meetings with each employee to discuss past performance and the specific goals each individual should focus on; to request a written plan from the employee, proposing sales goals and objectives appropriate for the upcoming period; to set a due date for the proposal submission and to schedule the next meeting for discussion and establishment of the sales goals.

3. After examining each employee's proposal, the sales manager meets for the second time with each employee, to

discuss the proposal, to obtain agreement with the manager's modifications, and to assign actual sales goals for the following period. Surprisingly, most managers find that each individual's proposed sales goals are often 10 to 20 percent higher than the level the manager would have assigned.

4. When the goals have been mutually agreed on, the manager puts them into writing and both the employee and manager sign these written goals. Signing further increases ownership of the goals by both the employee and manager, and increases the probability of meeting or exceeding them.

5. Steps 2 through 4 are repeated before each new period, to establish sales goals for each employee.

❏ AVOIDING AVERAGE PERFORMANCE INDIFFERENCE

Bank managers usually have little difficulty identifying their best and worst performers; the difficulty lies in ranking the middle layer of average performers. Because these average performers typically represent 80 to 85 percent of all bank employees, the performance of this group greatly affects the bank's sales culture, quality of service, and, ultimately, its financial performance.

When the bank cannot rank this middle layer, it unwittingly becomes indifferent to varying levels of performance within an average range. To make things worse, managers have a natural tendency to spread out raises evenly to most members of this group, discouraging the better employees in the group and encouraging the poorer ones to continue their mediocre performance. It is imperative that this group be ranked to spur competition and motivation. Unfortunately, most banks do not attempt to rank average performers, and there is little or no incentive to improve within this group. One bank's strategy to improve its average performers follows:

We knew that to successfully improve the performance of our average employees, we needed to evaluate and *rank* each against the others based on performance. First, approximate rankings are determined by performance appraisals. Then, a committee of managers meets and begins ranking the employees individually against each other, taking two employees at a time. This process is computer-assisted. Our managers continue ranking the employees against each other in pairs until a definite ranking is established and then posted for the entire group. Based on the ranking raises and promotions are awarded and career paths decided. We have been amazed at how motivated our average employees have become, now that they realize that they will be ranked and rewarded based on their performance compared to their peers.

❏ BUILDING ESTEEM FOR SALES POSITIONS

In large public accounting firms, an accountant must often work for years, and rise to the rank of partner, before being allowed to make that first sales call. Most investment banks allow only their most senior and experienced officers to make sales calls and presentations to prospective clients. Needless to say, the right to represent the firm and make sales calls is viewed as an honor within these firms.

Several banks use this same principle successfully by structuring positions that require their employees to earn the right to represent the bank. Employees must meet established levels of product knowledge and sales skill proficiency before being allowed to either sell or earn incentives. Only the most successful employees, on both the wholesale and retail sides, are allowed to make sales calls or engage in selling. The effectiveness and frequency of sales calls made at these banks, especially at the senior levels, are dramatically higher than at average-performance banks.

❏ DEVELOPING TARGET ACCOUNTS

Quarterly, individual relationship managers should develop a list of *both* target customers and noncustomer prospects. For target customers, sales goals should include increasing either the volume or breadth of the services used. For prospects, specific goals should be established for the types of services and volume level sold during the next quarter. Management should evaluate the relationship managers on the success and percentage of target customers and prospects converted. Limiting the target list to under ten prospects or customers allows relationship managers to sufficiently focus on each target and to produce visible results.

❏ INCREASING AVAILABLE SALES TIME

Time studies often highlight bottlenecks that can be avoided by modifying existing duties, operational procedures, organizational structures, and responsibilities. Although time allocation differs greatly between banks, Figure 3–1 on the following page shows common officer activity times. Note that most commercial calling officers and branch managers devote only 10 to 20 percent of their total available time to sales or sales management activity. A mere 5 percent increase in total time spent on sales activities equates to a 25 to 50 percent increase in overall sales effort and yields a substantial improvement in results. In a few banks, this 5 percent of total time cannot be identified and channeled to selling activities. Here is one bank's experience:

> Our managers and line officers are continually being asked to do more work. When we asked them to set aside additional time for selling activities, most responded that they did not have any remaining time to devote to sales or sales management. We realized that in order to expect our officers and managers to increase their sales efforts, they must first be convinced that they have the time available. By performing a basic time study of our employees, we were able to pinpoint where time was being spent. By presenting internal time study results to our employees and jointly deciding which nonsales activities could be decreased, we were able to achieve acceptance and buy-in, to increase the amount of time dedicated to business development and sales activity.

COMMERCIAL CALLING OFFICERS
AVERAGE TIME SPENT BY FUNCTION

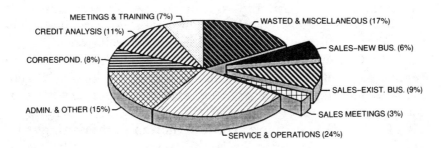

MEETINGS & TRAINING (7%)
CREDIT ANALYSIS (11%)
CORRESPOND. (8%)
ADMIN. & OTHER (15%)
WASTED & MISCELLANEOUS (17%)
SALES–NEW BUS. (6%)
SALES–EXIST. BUS. (9%)
SALES MEETINGS (3%)
SERVICE & OPERATIONS (24%)

BRANCH MANAGERS
AVERAGE TIME SPENT BY FUNCTION

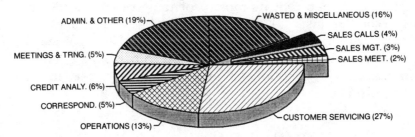

ADMIN. & OTHER (19%)
MEETINGS & TRNG. (5%)
CREDIT ANALY. (6%)
CORRESPOND. (5%)
OPERATIONS (13%)
WASTED & MISCELLANEOUS (16%)
SALES CALLS (4%)
SALES MGT. (3%)
SALES MEET. (2%)
CUSTOMER SERVICING (27%)

Figure 3–1 Relationship Manager Time Management Graphs (Source: Independent research survey to heads of commercial and retail banking within leading international banks, 6/89, n = 300, error margin +/−4%.)

❏ FOCUSING CALLING EFFORT

Because of the high cost of sales calls, a significant increase in profitability can be achieved by focusing relationship manager time on the most profitable existing and potential business. To accomplish this task, a bank must be able to analyze its wholesale customer base by individual customer relationship profitability. Once that profitability is calculated, the accounts are separated by industry type, sales revenue, credit needs, geographic location, and any other criteria that marketing or management suspects might affect relationship profitability. This study should be more accurate than most marketing studies, because relationship profitability should be fully loaded (see the section on "Relationship Profitability Model Development," on page 61).

Once management has determined which criteria lead to profitable relationships, officer calling time can be increased, decreased, or redirected, to maximize the bank's profitability. The relationship profitability graph in Figure 3–2 on the following page is a generic example. The bank represented in the graph determined that its most profitable relationships originated from "Industry D" companies that had a certain range of sales revenue per year. A prospect list of all companies that met the stated criteria was distributed to the bank's relationship managers for follow-up and special emphasis in their calling efforts.

❏ FOCUSING CALLING TALENT

To maximize the revenues generated from the bank's most profitable existing and potential customers, sales management must systematically align the bank's most effective and talented relationship managers and branch managers with its most profitable customers. This approach can ensure top quality coverage of its key accounts. Here is how one bank did it:

> We did not want to suddenly change the account assignments of our relationship managers, especially where an existing officer had a

RELATIONSHIP PROFITABILITY BY INDUSTRY

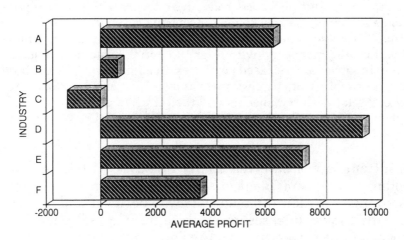

INDUSTRY D RELATIONSHIP PROFIT BY SALES

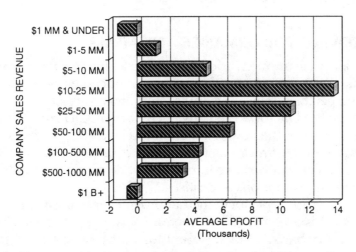

Figure 3-2 Relationship Profitability Graphs (Source: Sample illustration of corporate banking profitability by industry then revenue.)

strong relationship with a profitable client. However, we did want to gradually align our most productive officers with our most profitable accounts, in order to maximize bank revenue. We decided to establish a systematic process that would match top performing relationship managers with high potential customers selected from inquiries and released portfolios. In addition, we ranked both the profitability of our customers and the perceived performance of our relationship managers and then drafted a model list of accounts within each relationship manager's portfolio. We strive to replicate this model list over time.

Not all employees have the ability or desire to become outstanding relationship managers, nor is it necessarily desirable to terminate relationship managers who perform well in areas other than sales. In cases where sales training, sales management attention, incentives, and rewards fail to produce high-performance relationship managers, portfolio responsibilities and job positions must be shifted if the bank wishes to retain these employees because of their other skills.

☐ IMPROVING PERFORMANCE APPRAISALS

An essential measurement tool is the performance appraisal (PA). If management is to emphasize the importance of a sales culture, the performance appraisal system must reflect sales as a heavily weighted factor. When any necessary modification has been done, a copy of the new criteria should be distributed to all employees. The employees must realize that sales achievement will become a critical variable in performance appraisal results and subsequent promotions and raises.

An excerpt from a performance appraisal form is shown in Figure 3–3. This excerpt is not meant to represent the ideal format for every bank. Many different formats can be effective. It does, however, illustrate how detailed and specific sales goals can be described and measured.

COMMERCIAL BANKING PERFORMANCE APPRAISAL

Name: John Q. Public   Salary Grade: _____

Title: Assistant Vice President   Date: _____

Area: Commercial Lending   SSN: _____

Review Period: From _____ To _____

Instructions: The employee should first state the specific performance goals that have been projected for the upcoming review period in each "Objective" area. All individuals must identify at least eight objectives including #9 and #10. #11 & #12 are required for officers with supervisory responsibility. A maximum of twelve identifiable goals is acceptable. Objectives should be quantified, whenever possible, in terms of dollars, target dates, or volumes. Each objective must then be approved by the immediate supervisor who will assign a weighting according to the perceived difficulty in achieving that goal. Goals considered in the bottom 25% of perceived difficulty should receive a .9 weighting, those in the middle 50% should receive a 1.0 weighting, and those goals which are in the top 25% according to achievement difficulty should receive a 1.1 weighting. The employee and supervisor should jointly determine the overall importance of each objective as a percentage of total goals identified, with the total accumulating to 100%. Once objectives have been finalized and their weights and percentages are set, both the employee and the supervisor should indicate their approval by signing the form. At the end of the review period, the supervisor shall determine the achievement of each objective in the "achievement" area and rate that goal achievement on a zero to five scale (see end of form for scale key). Finally, total points for each objective will be assessed and tallied under the box marked "Total Points." The appropriate performance level will be assigned according to the number of points earned. Any revision of objectives should be documented, and all information on this form should be typed legibly.

---

1. OBJECTIVE: Increase average YTD loans outstanding by 22%, minimum yield on aggregate outstandings of Base + .50%. Maintain net interest margin on total portfolio of 4.05%, or minimum net interest income of $260,000 for the year (Q1-$60K, Q2-$70K, Q3-$55K, Q4-$75K).

1. ACHIEVEMENT: Q1-$62K, Q2-$68K, Q3-$70K, Q4-$88K. Loan portfolio grew at average YTD rate of 26.5%. Net interest income totaled $288K.

WEIGHT: 1.1   PERCENTAGE: 30%   RATING: 4   TOTAL: 132

Figure 3–3 Performance Appraisal Excerpt (Commercial Example)

2. OBJECTIVE: Increase YTD average checking balances by a minimum of 15%. Goal: YTD average collected checking balances of $3.4 million at year end.

2. ACHIEVEMENT: Q1-$3.2M, Q2-$3.0M, Q3-$2.6M, Q4-$3.2M. YTD average checking collected balance of $3.0M. XYZ Corp. moved its total relationship with average collected balance of $375K to United Jersey following LBO of XYZ.

WEIGHT: 1.0   PERCENTAGE: 20%   RATING: 2   TOTAL: 40

3. OBJECTIVE: Generate loan fee income of $20,750 and non-credit fee income of $29,250 (Q1-$13K, Q2-$12K, Q3-$10K, Q4-$15K).

3. ACHIEVEMENT: Q1-$13.2K, Q2-$12.8K, Q3-$11.7K, Q4-$12.2K. Loan fee income generated $22,040. Non-credit fee income of $27,880.

WEIGHT: 1.0   PERCENTAGE: 10%   RATING: 3   TOTAL: 30

9. OBJECTIVE: DEVELOPMENT OF FUNCTIONAL SKILLS (Consider efforts to acquire additional skills or further develop existing ones necessary for the job). Attend minimum of three days in sales training and five days in credit training seminars and classes. This should include one outside bank seminar on advanced credit techniques or corporate finance techniques for no more than three work days.

9. ACHIEVEMENT: Attended eight days of training including six days of in-house seminars and one two-day seminar on advanced credit skills.

WEIGHT: 1.0   PERCENTAGE: 15%   RATING: 3   TOTAL: 45

Figure 3-3   (continued)

10. OBJECTIVE: PLANNING AND CONTROL (Consider performance results in terms of accuracy in budgeting, work priorities, and effective use of time). Spend at least three days per week in customer and prospect identification. Concentrate on development and follow-up of new business opportunities. Keep within personal business expense budget goals.

10. ACHIEVEMENT: Spent more time in customer identification and prospect identification. Stayed within personal business expense goals.

WEIGHT: 1.0   PERCENTAGE: 5%   RATING: 3   TOTAL: 15

For Officers with Manager Responsibilities:

11. OBJECTIVE: DEVELOPMENT OF PEOPLE (Consider progress in developing subordinates, delegation of power and training effectiveness).

11. ACHIEVEMENT:

WEIGHT: PERCENTAGE: RATING: TOTAL:

12. OBJECTIVE: LEADERSHIP (Consider officer's ability to motivate and communicate with subordinates).

12. ACHIEVEMENT:

WEIGHT: PERCENTAGE: RATING: TOTAL:

| | EVALUATION CRITERIA | | SCALE | |
RATING	QUANTITATIVE (%)	QUALITATIVE	TOTAL POINTS	PERFORMANCE
5	More than 125%	Distinguished	500–550	Five
4	110–124%	Excellent	400–499	Four
3	100–109%	Good	300–399	Three
2	86–99%	Adequate	200–299	Two
1	76–85%	Marginal	100–199	One
0	75 or less	Unacceptable	99 or below	Zero

TOTAL POINTS: _____   PERFORMANCE: _____

Source: Adapted by permission of UJB Financial, Princeton, New Jersey.

Figure 3–3 (*continued*)

❏ EVALUATING PERFORMANCE MEASUREMENT CRITERIA

The number of employee performance goals that can be measured is almost infinite. It is critical to choose goals that fit well into the bank's strategic objectives. These goals should be easily tracked and understood by the employees being evaluated. Simplicity in design and understanding are essential. Frequently measured goals are shown in Table 3–2.

❏ ENHANCING CROSS-SELL MEASUREMENT

A bank's greatest potential for increased profit lies in its existing customer base. Unfortunately, the measurement of cross-sell ratios often has the negative impact of reducing the sales effort made to existing customers. Emphasis on selling to existing customers will often cause a platform representative's cross-sell ratio to plummet because it typically results in single product addition. For this reason, a number of high-performance banks measure existing and new customer cross-sell ratios separately.

When bankwide competitions are based on cross-sell ratios, some banks have found it necessary to weight cross-sell ratios in specific branches because of their locations near industrial complexes, in high-growth communities, or in population-intensive neighborhoods. Cross-sell ratios can often be abnormally high in these branches, regardless of platform representatives' true abilities or efforts. The results often discourage platform representatives in branches that have no demographic biases. By weighting performance levels based on past historical data, managers ensure an even playing field in which actual effort and skill are more accurately measured.

Another weakness of many cross-sell measurement systems is their inability to differentiate between sales of profitable and unprofitable products. This deficiency often inspires platform representatives to focus on "easy sells" while hardly ever selling more profitable products. Such a focus is especially damaging when a customer needs a more profitable product but the platform representative is uncomfortable either identifying the need or selling unfamiliar products.

Table 3–2 Frequently Measured Employee Goals

Branch Managers:

Loan growth (separate commercial, if applicable).

Deposit growth (only if platform representatives also compensated).

New loan and deposit volumes.

Overall branch profitability goals.

Customer defection rates.

Profitability of individual loans.

Total product profitability (products weighted by profitability and summed).

Charge-off goals.

Volume of business development calls.

New business development goals.

Employee-turnover reduction goals.

Service and fee-income goals.

Total platform representative performance (by cross-sell or other measurement).

Special product promotion goals.

Referrals to commercial, trust, private banking, etc.

Total product volume goals.

Total customer volume goals.

Total teller performance and referrals.

Customer satisfaction goals (by survey).

Expense goals.

Penetration ratio (per product).

Side product goals (e.g., disability loan insurance).

Meeting goals in a certain number of total categorized products.

Key customer shift.

Aging analysis.

Average products per customer or household.

Average dollars per household.

Table 3–2 (*continued*)

Platform Representatives:

Customer volume (increases contacts per time unit).

Assigned key customer increase or profitability.

Profitability of individual products sold.

Cross-sell ratios (increases efficiency per contact).

Customer satisfaction rate (by survey).

Customer defection rate.

Fee-income goals.

Service proficiency (by shoppers, if applicable).

Referrals to trust, commercial, private banking, etc.

Special product promotion goals.

Meeting goals in a certain number of total categorized products.

Time deposit rollover volume.

Efficiency/error percentages.

New accounts (new funds, new households).

Commercial Officers:

Loan growth goals (both volume and quality).

Deposit growth goals.

Charge-off goals.

Total portfolio profitability goals.

Customer defection rates.

Profitability of specific targeted clients.

Volume of business development calls.

Volume of total customers and accounts.

New fund and new loan goals.

Meeting goals in a certain number of total categorized products.

Expense goals.

Table 3-2 (*continued*)

Penetration ratio (per product and per account).
Closing ratio (per call).
Cross-sell volume or ratio (i.e., cash management, etc.).
Fee-income generation.
Customer satisfaction (by survey).
Referral goals to retail, trust, etc.
Average products and deposits per client.

Department Managers:

Profitability of area managed.
Volume of total customers and accounts.
Volume of customers serviced.
Customer defection rates.
Service proficiency.
Average penetration ratios by account and product.
Percentage of subordinate incentives.
New fund and new loan goals.
Employee turnover reduction goals.
Employees meeting goals in multiple product categories.
Referral goals by the area.
Customer satisfaction goals by the area.
Expense goals.
Growth in market share.
Fee-income generation by the area.
Deposit increases by area (if applic.).
Loan volume increases by area (if applic.).

To solve this problem, several high-performance banks weight products according to their approximate profit contributions. The platform representative is then more willing to present the relevant product when the need is uncovered. Additional weighting also makes it worthwhile for platform representatives to become familiar with more products and to gain the ability to sell them effectively.

❑ RETAIL DEPOSIT GROWTH AND REFERRAL CREDIT

To increase the referral volume from the branches to the trust, private banking or commercial areas, dual accreditation, in terms of performance measurements and incentives, for deposits and revenues generated from the referrals must be given to both areas. Not to do so will lead to the blocking of any referrals that improve bank profitability but decrease the perceived performance of any branch or department.

❑ ESTABLISHING A SALES APPROACH BY BUSINESS UNIT

Most marketing and sales literature claims that a *customer-based* approach (the selling of services based on individual customer needs) is preferred and is more profitable than a *product-based* approach (selling products without identifying each individual customer's needs). Banking is the sum of many different businesses, each with its own unique markets and products. A close examination of high-performance banks indicates that a mixed strategy is the most profitable. In one example, a highly profitable credit card business unit (which became the largest issuer of Gold MasterCards) decided to focus on a purely product-based approach for marketing and selling its credit card services. Its training manual clearly stated that it was a product-based sales organization. The unequaled success of this unit demonstrates clearly that a bank should have a mixed approach, dependent on the nature and types of products and services offered by each strategic business unit.

❏ CONVERTING COMPETITIVE STRATEGY INTO TARGET MARKET STRATEGY

Competitive strategy is a key to the long-term performance of any bank. Table 3–3 lists basic competitive strategies used successfully in many high-performance banks. Competitive strategy must ultimately be converted into specific target market strategies that allow a bank to maximize its profitability and effectiveness in each market in which it operates. Table 3–4 illustrates a commercial middle-market example of the basic strategies some banks have chosen for targeting their customers.

❏ RELATIONSHIP MANAGER CROSS-SELL AND REFERRAL GOALS

Many banks have not formalized relationship manager goals and performance standards for cross-sell ratios, or quotas for such specific products as cash management products and other fee-generating products. In addition, many banks do not have standards for the number of referrals to trust, private banking, and other areas of the bank. Goals should be established and incentives set up where appropriate.

❏ TELLER REFERRAL GOALS

It is important to revise teller job descriptions and performance appraisals to include referral standards. Each bank must make its own decision about whether to offer monetary referral bonuses, but all should require *at least* two referrals per week from a full-time teller. If tellers have an incentive to make referrals, many banks will have initially paid out for them, whether or not they result in sales; but once the tellers become accustomed to making referrals, the banks can limit payout to only those referrals that result in sales. Most banks, initially wary of giving incentives to tellers for fear of slower service, have been pleasantly surprised. In almost every case, the tellers limited their selling activity during peak times and

Table 3-3 Basic Competitive Market Strategies

Strategies for Leading and Dominant Banks

Keep-the-Offensive Strategy—Keeping the initiative, and setting standards that rivals must meet.

Hold-and Maintain Strategy—Building a defense that makes it harder for underdog banks to attack.

Competitive Harassment Strategy—Retaliating for any challenge with massive countermeasures.

Increase Value-Added Through Integration—Integrating selectively to offer a wider array of services.

Operate Formula Facilities—Achieving low cost by standardizing facilities and operating efficiently.

Strategies for Underdogs or (SBUs) of Dominant Banks

Specialize by Product Type—Focusing on specialization in a specific product type.

Specialize by Customer Type—Catering to specific customer type.

Vacant-Niche Strategy—Concentrating on customers/products that competitors have bypassed or neglected.

No Frills Posture—Maintaining a lean operation based on low overhead and budget, to play intense price competition.

"Ours-Is-Better-Than-Theirs" Strategy—Focusing on marketing products with more features than competitors'.

Content-Follower Strategy—Offering products similar to those of leading banks, without direct confrontation.

Guppy Strategy—Seeking market share aggressively at the expense of smaller, weaker banks.

Distinctive-Image Strategy—Keeping high visibility by offering prestige quality, superior service, etc.

Harvest-to-Sell Strategy—Maximizing short-term profits and share prices, to attract buyers.

Table 3–3 (continued)

Questionable Bank Strategies

Copy-Cat Strategy—Imitating the strategy of a successful competitor bank.

Take-Away Strategy—Attacking other banks head-on, by lower prices, more advertising, and promotions.

Glamour Strategy—Depending on a new product or technology, without expertise or needed resources.

Test-the-Water Strategy—Adopting a halfway strategy that lacks adequate corporate commitment.

Hit-Another-Home-Run Strategy—Trying to repeat a successful strategy with a new product or market.

Arms-Race Strategy—Battling with major competitors to match price cuts, features, R & D, etc.

Drift Strategy—Reacting at the operating level day-to-day rather than having a conscious strategy.

Hope-for-a-Better-Day Strategy—Stating an unclear strategy until "good times" arrive.

Losing-Hand Strategy—Refusing to reformulate a previously (but no longer) successful strategy.

Popgun Strategy—Attempting to compete head-to-head against leaders, without resources or advantage.

Sources: Adapted from Philip Kotler, *Marketing Management,* 2d ed. (Englewood Cliffs, NJ: Prentice-Hall, 1972) Chap.8; and Joel Ross & Michael Kami, *Corporate Management in Crisis, Why the Mighty Fall* (Englewood Cliffs, NJ: Prentice-Hall, 1973).

Table 3–4   Basic Middle-Market Sales Strategies

Emerging Middle Market (Closely Held Business) Sales Strategies

Characteristics:

Single bank relationship and often underbanked.

Multiple calls and education of customers necessary.

Sales revenues inaccurate gauge of profit potential; industry type more relevant.

Prime targets: underbanked yet profitable partnerships, proprietorships, and closely held incorporated entities with single decision makers (no strong financial administrators) seeking hands-on financial servicing by a single bank.

Few new walk-in business customers; effective on-site calling is crucial to success.

Friendly reception by business owners and strong loyalty once the relationship begins.

Strategies:

Strive to capture lead (or sole) bank relationship with profitable, rapid-growth small companies with aggressive calling and marketing programs.

Specialization by industry type gains market share (i.e., physicians, lawyers, contractors, developers, insurance and financial firms, etc.).

The margin contribution of balances in small businesses is a greater portion of total customer profitability than middle-market and large corporate relationships. Deposits should be an equal or grater priority than credit services.

Selectivity by profitability "hurdle rates" ensures some profitability from the start.

Potential prospects should be screened for the potential of a long-term relationship, because account acquisition and calling force costs severely dilute initial profitability.

Table 3–4 *(continued)*

Recommended Sales Structure:

Specialized dedicated calling officers in demographically concentrated areas, in combination with decentralized branch
manager calling in remote areas where dedicated calling officers would not be cost-effective (branch managers are often
inundated by the product knowledge and repeat calls necessary to identify customer needs and sell noncredit products).
Branch managers with calling responsibilities should be assigned aggressive deposit goals, to partially compensate for
inherent disadvantage in selling other services.

Previous financial planners and private bankers perform above
average when hired. Redeployed large corporate and middle-
market lender are also good candidates.

Prime Middle-Market Sales Strategies

Characteristics:

Two or more banking relationships.

Need for basic trust, cash management, and credit services.

Strategies:

Reprice products and services for the bottom 10 to 20% of
customers, in terms of relationship profitability *each year.*

Selectively abandon highly price-sensitive customers where
the bank is not earning a fair rate of return and future potential for increased margins is doubtful.

Substantially decrease new business development calling efforts to upper-middle-market sectors, except for targeted
industries where margin hurdle rates can be met.

Concentrate calling focus on selling new services to existing
relationships instead of business development.

Table 3–4 (*continued*)

Give deposit capturing and fee-based services priority over lending.

Focus business development on companies that have a high probability of moving from a secondary to a lead bank relationship in a small amount of time, or on opportunistic events (i.e., where the potential customer has voiced dissatisfaction with its existing lead bank relationship, etc.) Strategies should be in place to expedite capturing the lead bank relationship.

Increase the bundling of services, to discourage price-sensitive customers from shopping the market to find the lowest prices available on each product used.

Specialize by industry type and "micro-markets," to improve market share.

Screen potential prospects for the potential of a long-term relationship, because account acquisition and calling force costs severely dilute initial profitability.

Recommended Sales Structure:

True relationship managers assigned to the bank's key accounts for the purpose of adjusting pricing and product mixes to maximize profitability.

Source: Council on Financial Competition. *Profit Strategies for the Middle Market* Washington: The Advisory Board, 1986, pp. 4–42.

reverted to selling during off-peak times, without the need to be coached by management.

A verifiable tracking system that monitors the level of referrals generated should be established. A system of transferring referral levels and referral quality into performance evaluations should also be in place. Rewards must be significant, to ensure continued improvement.

❑ PRODUCT GROUPING GOALS

Instituting *product grouping goals* ensures the widest possible selling depth across all products. In a typical plan, products are grouped together into similar categories and quotas are assigned for each category. To earn incentives, the relationship managers, branch managers, or platform representatives must reach their quotas in a certain number of the total categories. Product grouping differs from product bundling, which is a formal offer to the customer of a bundle of products, often at a discount. Product grouping ensures that each person attempts to sell all relevant bank services instead of focusing only on familiar products. One bank reports this experience with it:

> Although our sales numbers were solid in both commercial and retail areas, our product depth left much to be desired. In our retail area, both branch managers and platform representatives were simply selling their old standbys and rarely attempting to sell more lucrative products. In our commercial area, our push toward increasing noninterest income began to stall. Assigning product grouping goals changed this. In both commercial and retail areas, we began to see a significant increase in the depth of the products sold. Our officers and platform representatives knew that they had to sell a greater variety of products in order to be eligible for incentives.

❑ RELATIONSHIP PROFITABILITY MODEL DEVELOPMENT

A number of banks have successfully developed customer profitability models to quantify profitability per product and per customer. Revenues from interest income, compensating balance revenue, fees, and so on, are relatively simple to track. Some expenses require time studies to approximate where to allocate certain costs. To allocate such costs as overhead, relationship manager time, and servicing costs among wholesale customers, banks often implement 3-month time studies. Profitability models must also make provisions for customers who use multiple services, by reducing the allocation of fixed costs per product. Profitability models should be fully loaded and should therefore include the following costs (allocated directly, by management, by expert opinion, or by time studies):

- Administrative expenses
- Relationship manager time (both sales and account maintenance)
- Analysis and processing
- Risk adjustments or loss provisions
- All miscellaneous overhead (branch or facility costs, etc.)
- Servicing and other associated direct costs
- Cost of funds
- Miscellaneous acquisition costs
- Other costs.

Developing a meaningful customer profitability model can be challenging, especially for data collection, analysis, allocation, and presentation. A number of high-performance banks have found it worthwhile to purchase or develop sophisticated software programs that relate profitability to pricing, portfolio management, market analysis, and business development.

❏ ENCOURAGING RELATIONSHIP PRICING

Banks have relatively high fixed costs per customer acquisition. Increasing the volume of services per customer allows the bank to spread acquisition costs among multiple services, resulting in a lower cost per service provided and higher profitability per relationship. Lower costs per service allow a bank to pass savings to the customer through relationship pricing while still increasing overall profitability. Multiple accounts also improve customer loyalty and retention, increasing the net present value of each customer's worth.

Relationship pricing applies to more than the use of multiple services. Many banks also offer volume discounts for borrowing rates on funds over a certain threshold. This offer provides customers with incentives to engage in more business with a single bank. Relationship pricing effectively reduces price shopping by companies and consumers who use multiple financial institutions, choosing each for its lowest priced service (often a loss leader used to attract customers). Uncontrolled price shoppers are detrimental to bank earnings.

The complexity and automation levels needed to accurately determine individual relationship profitability have discouraged most banks from pricing their services on an individual basis. However, a number of banks have focused effectively on the top 10 to 25 percent of their retail and wholesale customer bases. Relationship pricing should not automatically be extended to a bank's best customers. Banks that have implemented relationship pricing successfully have used it as a sales tool, offering relationship pricing only to retain top customers in competitive situations or to attract new business from customers who can provide increased activity if given favorable pricing incentives.

4

Staffing Sales Performers

In the long term, hiring and retaining top sales performers will play a vital role in the development of a second-generation sales culture. The importance of proper staffing can be seen by calculating the potential revenue lost because of the poor salesmanship of a relationship manager throughout his or her employment tenure. Add to this total the cost of hiring, relocating, and training a replacement, and the revenue lost until the new trainee becomes effective. Then multiply this new total by the number of relationship managers who do not presently exceed revenue expectations. The actual cost can be staggering. Human resources officers and managers must become skilled at determining specific traits, attributes, and backgrounds that produce top sales performers. All interviewing and selection methods must be tailored to hiring the right candidates. The ideas described in this chapter have proved highly effective.

❏ SALES TEST SCREENING

Sales test screening can improve the odds of hiring a high-performance sales candidate. Sales tests provide a strong indicator of future sales performance. They identify high-risk applicants, decrease relationship manager and sales staff turnover, pinpoint candidate weakness areas for remedial training if hired, and increase the probability of a good cultural fit. (See Figure 4–1 for a sample sales test.) Not using sales test screening for all positions with sales responsibilities can be an expensive mistake. One bank's experience with sales test screening reinforces that warning:

> At first we were skeptical of the value of sales screening tests. However, after discussions with several testing services, we began to screen platform representative candidates. To determine whether the screening tests would cost justify themselves, we decided to test every other qualified applicant, in order to build a control group for later analysis. After placing the system into service for approximately 6 months, we noticed significantly higher cross-sell ratios and slightly lower turnover rates among the platform representatives who were exposed to the sales screening and tested positively. At that point, we adopted sales screening tests on a mandatory basis for all sales positions, both wholesale and retail. To our pleasant surprise, we found an even higher correlation between sales performance and test results with our relationship managers and branch managers. It would be unthinkable for us to ever revert back to our original hiring practices, which did not include sales test screening.

❑ APPLICANT ROLE PLAYING

A popular technique among sales managers in other industries is to ask applicants to sell during the interview. Role playing can be easily implemented if they provide an applicant with a description or product profile of the bank's products, as well as an imaginary but lifelike scenario. The applicant is usually given 15 to 30 minutes alone, to study the information. The applicant then attempts to sell the product to the potential customer (interviewer). The interviewer has a first-hand opportunity to view the applicant's initial abilities in building rapport, empathizing, retention, use of product knowledge, and other crucial sales abilities. Despite its effectiveness during an interview, many banks with average or low-performance sales cultures still do not use role playing on a regular basis.

Section I

1. How old were you when you started your first job, such as paper routing, baby sitting, lawn mowing, etc.?
   a. Not employed prior to full-time work
   b. 9 years or less
   c. 10 to 12 years
   d. 13 to 15 years
   e. 16 to 18 years
   f. 19 to 21 years
   g. 22 years or more
2. How did you get your current job, or your last job if now unemployed?
   a. Have never been employed
   b. Through a friend or relative
   c. Through a contact from a previous job
   d. I contacted the employer
   e. The employer contacted me
   f. Through an employment agency or bureau
   g. By answering an advertisement
   h. Some other way
3. How many full-time jobs have you held in the past five years?
   a. None
   b. 1
   c. 2
   d. 3
   e. 4
   f. 5
   g. 6 or more
4. What was your average length of employment in all your previous full-time jobs?
   a. Have never been employed full-time
   b. Less than one year
   c. 1 but less than 2 years
   d. 2 but less than 4 years
   e. 4 but less than 7 years
   f. 7 but less than 10 years
   g. 10 years or more
5. Between the time you left your last job and the time you applied for this job, how long were you out of work?
   a. Was employed when I applied
   b. Less than 1 month
   c. 1 but less than 6 months
   d. 6 months or more
   e. No previous job
6. How adequate is the income you receive from your current job?
   a. No Current job
   b. Not adequate to provide minimum essentials
   c. Just adequate to provide minimum essentials
   d. Adequate for a decent standard of living
   e. More than adequate to live on comfortably

Figure 4–1   Sales Aptitude Test

7. Of the following, which one is the most important reason you are thinking of changing jobs?
    a. This will be my first full-time job
    b. I was or will be laid off or terminated
    c. I need more income
    d. Little or no opportunity in present job
    e. I do not like my present job
    f. I do not like my boss or co-workers
    g. I want to change careers
    h. I am relocating
    i. Some other reason

8. How much experience in selling or sales have you had?
    a. I have never held a sales position
    b. Part-time occasional basis only
    c. 6 months but less than 1 year
    d. 1 year but less than 18 months
    e. 18 months but less than 2 years
    f. 2 years but less than 3 years
    g. 3 years but less than 5 years
    h. 5 years or more

9. How much experience have you had selling financial products, mutual funds, stocks and bonds, other securities?
    a. I have never held a sales position
    b. Part-time occasional basis only
    c. 6 months but less than 1 year
    d. 1 year but less than 18 months
    e. 18 months but less than 2 years
    f. 2 years but less than 3 years
    g. 3 years but less than 5 years
    h. 5 years or more

10. What is your highest level of education?
    a. Did not graduate high school
    b. High school graduate or equivalent
    c. 1 year college completed
    d. 2 years college completed
    e. 3 years college completed
    f. College graduate
    g. Some graduate school (must be col. grad.)
    h. Graduate school degree

11. What percent of your college education—room, board, tuition, spending money—did you finance through your own efforts? (Consider scholarships, loans, ROTC, jobs, etc.)
    a. Did not go to college
    b. Less than 10%
    c. 10 to 25%
    d. 26 to 50%
    e. 51 to 75%
    f. 76 to 100%

Figure 4–1 (continued)

<table>
</table>

Section II

KEY: I AM . . .
- a. Not at all concerned
- b. Slightly concerned
- c. Moderately concerned
- d. Highly concerned

12. Being able to meet the expectations of management.
    a b c d
13. Being able to find enough clients
    a b c d
14. Being able to accept rejection by potential buyers
    a b c d
15. Having too little time to spend with family and friends
    a b c d
16. Being accepted as a financial advisor
    a b c d
17. Being able to get along with the other sales representatives and coworkers
    a b c d
18. Being able to do the job to meet my standards
    a b c d
19. Being able to learn all the product knowledge necessary
    a b c d
20. Mixing abusiness with pleasure at social events, club meetings, etc.
    a b c d
21. Approaching friends and acquaintances for business purposes
    a b c d
22. Making presentations to committees of senior people in a company
    a b c d
23. Approaching senior business officers whom I have never met before
    a b c d
24. Having to use the tlelphone to obtain clients
    a b c d

KEY:
- a. Not at all
- b. A little
- c. Somewhat
- d. Moderately
- e. Definitely

OTHERS SEE ME AS:
25. risk taker   a b c d e
26. dissatisfied   a b c d e
27. disciplined   a b c d e
28. entertaining   a b c d e
29. aggressive   a b c d e
30. impatient   a b c d e
31. impulsive   a b c d e
32. quiet   a b c d e
33. precise   a b c d e
34. secretive   a b c d e
35. persuasive   a b c d e
36. active   a b c d e

Figure 4–1 (continued)

37.	direct	a	b	c	d	e
38.	selfless	a	b	c	d	e
39.	analytical	a	b	c	d	e
40.	changeable	a	b	c	d	e
41.	devoted	a	b	c	d	e
42.	resolute	a	b	c	d	e
43.	outgoing	a	b	c	d	e
44.	innovator	a	b	c	d	e
AS I REALLY AM:						
45.	risk taker	a	b	c	d	e
46.	dissatisfied	a	b	c	d	e
47.	disciplined	a	b	c	d	e
48.	entertaining	a	b	c	d	e
49.	aggressive	a	b	c	d	e
50.	impatient	a	b	c	d	e
51.	impulsive	a	b	c	d	e
52.	quiet	a	b	c	d	e
53.	precise	a	b	c	d	e
54.	secretive	a	b	c	d	e
55.	persuasive	a	b	c	d	e
56.	active	a	b	c	d	e
57	direct	a	b	c	d	e
58.	selfless	a	b	c	d	e
59.	analytical	a	b	c	d	e
60.	changeable	a	b	c	d	e
61.	devoted	a	b	c	d	e
62.	resolute	a	b	c	d	e
63.	outgoing	a	b	c	d	e
64.	innovator	a	b	c	d	e

On completion, please return this test to the individual who administered.

Source: Composite adapted by permission from a collection of 12 manufacturing and financial services firms' sales screening tests.

Figure 4–1 (*continued*)

❑ MODIFYING INTERVIEWING PROFILES

A crucial element in staffing sales performers is the modification of personality and experience profiles developed during the interviewing process. Most Human Resources executives strongly believe that past sales or similar experience is preferred and that a candidate's past sales performance, even if in another industry, is a strong indicator of future sales performance in banking. The more related the industry or market, the more predictive past performance has been. References provided by a candidate must clearly establish the candidate's past sales performance. In establishing personality profiles of candidates without sales experience, many banks look for traits of extreme self-confidence (ego strength), self-sufficiency, a track record of goal orientation, and empathy (the ability to relate to customers and their needs).

The ability to set goals before sales calls or meetings and then to accomplish those goals successfully is essential to top sales performance. One technique used by interviewers to test goal orientation during meetings is to shift from the subject at hand to an unrelated topic, first making a mental or written note of exactly the subject they had switched from and even the last few sentences mentioned on that topic. Many Human Resources professionals feel that, if the candidates remain on the nonrelated topic as long as the interviewer does not shift back, either the candidates are reciting what they think the interviewer wants to hear, or the candidates have little goal orientation, or both.

If a candidate politely switches to the interviewer's new topic momentarily and then reverts back to the relevant topic, the candidate likely has internal direction, focus, and goal orientation. If the candidate can revert back to the original topic and even paraphrase the last sentence or two on the relevant topic and can do so consistently, the candidate likely has extreme focus and at least one trait commonly found in sales superstars. Caution should be used, so as not to weight certain abilities too heavily in the interviewing process, and all factors should be taken into consideration before hiring the candidate.

❏ DUPLICATING TOP PERFORMERS

One way to increase the probability of hiring successful applicants is to identify the experience levels and traits that have led to success in the bank's existing high performers. A detailed job analysis is often done for each position by having the high performers and their managers draft a list of the traits and experiences they feel are most relevant in their success. Next, a master list is made from the individual lists and distributed to the participants, who rank each characteristic and its importance for success in a specific position. The bank has now a useful list of characteristics to help identify potential high performers during the interviewing process.

More importantly, the employees who are closest to the job and know the position best are the same individuals who have drafted the characteristics needed, in most cases ensuring a more accurate profile. The candidates who score highest on meeting the desired profile will often have the highest probability of success in the position for which they are interviewed and tested. An example of a Candidate Selection Profile is shown in Figure 4–2.

The next step in the process is to design various questions that interviewers can ask candidates, to determine the degree to which they meet each characteristic. If a bank is large enough and there are enough individuals in a specific position, the profile screening can be administered to existing employees, to verify the profile validity and to establish benchmark scores that identify top performers. Some banks have taken the candidate selection profile process even further by analyzing the trainable characteristics that candidates must possess initially. The interviewers then judge candidates only on those necessary characteristics. Identifying trainable skills also provides valuable feedback for the training area, which can then tailor a curriculum to provide the desired characteristics and skills.

❏ EFFECTIVE BACKGROUND CHECKS

The most accurate predictor of future performance is past performance; yet, few banks have mastered the art of effective background checks. References provided by candidates can be highly useful in nontraditional hiring screens. The references are selected by the candidate to provide positive comments and they probably will do so, regardless of the quality of the candidate. However, asking primary references for names of others familiar with the candidate's work patterns and performance provides uncensored secondary references who will often give an impartial view of the candidate's past performance and abilities. Other excellent secondary references would include past customers or accounts suggested by the candidate's primary references. What better sources of information on how your own customers will probably view the new employee? Do past customers think the candidate will succeed in the new position?

Name: _____ Applied Position: _____

Desired Characteristic Category	Job Importance (0–10)	Candidate Score (0–10)	Item Score	Category Score
Traits:				
_____	_____ ×	_____ =	_____	
_____	_____ ×	_____ =	_____	
_____	_____ ×	_____ =	_____	
_____	_____ ×	_____ =	_____	
_____	_____ ×	_____ =	_____	
_____	_____ ×	_____ =	_____	
_____	_____ ×	_____ =	_____	

Category Weight _____ (0–10) × Item Score Total _____ = _____

Skills:				
_____	_____ ×	_____ =	_____	
_____	_____ ×	_____ =	_____	
_____	_____ ×	_____ =	_____	

Category Weight _____ (0–10) × Item Score Total _____ = _____

Figure 4–2   Candidate Selection Profile

Desired Characteristic Category	Job Importance (0–10)	Candidate Score (0–10)	Item Score	Category Score
Education:				
_____	____ ×	____ =	____	
_____	____ ×	____ =	____	
Category Weight ____ (0–10) × Item Score Total ____ = ____				
Work Experience:				
_____	____ ×	____ =	____	
_____	____ ×	____ =	____	
_____	____ ×	____ =	____	
Category Weight ____ (0–10) × Item Score Total ____ = ____				
TOTAL CANDIDATE SCORE				____

Figure 4–2 (continued)

Would past customers buy again, if the candidate were selling a needed item, even if many other sources were available?

Ask all references to quantify the candidate's performance on a percentage basis without providing a frame of reference. References virtually always call a candidate "above average" during the course of a background interview. If they score the same candidate below 90 percent, however, the candidate was probably not the company's rising superstar.

Even if the position being recruited for does not require one, a credit check can be a valuable reflection of the candidate's life-style. Does the candidate always meet or exceed obligations? Is the candidate dependable? Does the candidate have problems that will not be met adequately by the company's tentative salary offer?

Tracking a candidate's past salary history can be revealing. Did the candidate's salary ever stagnate for more than a year? Was the salary ever reduced and, if so, was there a change in positions that would have made the salary cut worth the long-term potential? Were promotions to new positions matched by salary increases and were the increases substantial?

❑ SETTING ABSOLUTE HIRING STANDARDS

A bank can maintain a sustainable advantage over its competitors by doing a better job in hiring. Unfortunately, when most banks decide that they need to staff a position, they gather candidates through multiple channels, review résumés, interview several candidates, and then hire the best among these candidates. Although this method efficiently and predictably fills the vacancy, it is flawed in that it does not establish absolute standards, but simply awards a position to the best among mediocre candidates. The bank's employees then closely reflect the median quality of the available labor pool. A few top international companies hold out for absolute standards, often not hiring anyone unless that person is ideally suited for the position. High-performance banks should not settle for anything less. One top bank had this experience:

> Instead of only hiring when a position is open, we are always hiring. We spurn hiring the top mediocre candidate and instead establish absolute standards. We will hire an exceptionally qualified person even if the position is not open. In the long run, we win because we have assured ourselves an excellent candidate for a position that will eventually open and that person will likely perform well in other positions until the planned position becomes available.
>
> The new employees also win because they get a well-rounded background in other banking areas and in the corporate environment until the targeted position opens. Their learning curve when it

does open is reduced. We exercise caution, however, to ensure that the temporary position is challenging and exciting for the candidate, that the candidate has the proper background and skills to excel in the temporary position, and that the eventual position or its equivalent will be open within a reasonable period (often considered to be within 1 year).

The Human Resources area alone cannot maintain the bank's competitive advantage of employing superior workers. Responsibility should also fall on every bank manager. This responsibility should be spelled out in performance appraisals and reinforced through training and through the establishment of recruiting assistance objectives.

❏ BEATING OUT COMPETITORS FOR TOP GRADUATES

The options and choices available to most top college graduates make it a challenge to hire the best. Several banks systematically lock-in top students even before competitors have seen them. They use a nontraditional co-op hiring program.

Recruiting begins, toward the end of the target candidates' junior year, for a summer internship that offers an excellent hourly wage or salary. College professors are asked to make the summer internships known to their *best* students, and past interns are canvassed for candidate recommendations. If a greater number of high-quality minority students is needed, recruiting presentations at minority fraternities and sororities are often successful.

Once chosen, the candidates are sent to work and learn in various departments throughout the bank; they meet employees and build an allegiance to the bank. Performance and abilities are carefully monitored. The best interns are then offered permanent positions subject to graduation. The internship program assures top incoming management trainees. Reduced officer turnover is an additional benefit because the bank has had the opportunity to observe the candidates in a work environment before making the employment offer.

❏ RECRUITING COMPETING BANKS' STARS

Competitors can be a major source of talent and should not be ignored. Unfortunately, most unsolicited applicants who want to switch from a competitor are mismatches. Although mismatches sometimes develop because of shortcomings in a competitor's work environment, they usually happen when the applicant is unsuitable for the work at hand because of personality or ability conflicts. One leading bank's strategy is this:

> Despite mixed experience with unsolicited applicants, we regularly identify the very best relationship managers, branch managers, and other sales officers from competing organizations and recruit them aggressively. This is done by regularly questioning and interviewing our own relationship managers, wholesale customers, and applicants from competing banks for the names of these high performers. When appropriate openings develop, we contact these top performers discreetly and make them aware of the opening in a friendly, supportive way. We commonly offer sizable salaries and signing bonuses, because these candidates are usually far more productive than the average. Signing bonuses are contingent on a 2- to 3-year tenure, or they must be repaid. At worst, a relationship will be established with highly competent professionals who will remember our bank, should they wish to change positions at a later date. At best, a top performer will have been removed from a competitor's ranks and placed with the right bank.

❏ HIRING PAY STRATEGIES

One problem typically encountered when hiring for positions that include incentive pay is that incentives hurt the ability to recruit. Most candidates are wary of incentive pay and often choose to work for employers who offer the highest guaranteed salary. An effective way to get around this is to offer a high base salary for the first 6 to 12 months (or longer, if the training period dictates it). During this initial period, the candidates often do not have the ability to earn incentives. The candidates should be advised that, after the initial period, the base will drop or remain constant and the employee will then be eligible for incentive pay. This technique often eases the fears of a candidate in accepting a job with an uncertain pay level. Some banks also offer bonuses based on the performance appraisal of the trainee after 6 to 12 months.

❏ MODIFYING JOB DESCRIPTIONS

Most sales-oriented banks modify job descriptions to include and clearly describe sales responsibilities. Modifying job descriptions will emphasize to present employees that selling is an expected function and will attract sales-oriented job candidates.

❏ REVERSING RESIGNATIONS

Of equal importance to finding top performers is the task of retaining them. It is crucial that a bank train all managers to effectively deal with top performer resignations. The loss of experience, business relationships, proven performance, and potential business lost, and the cost of hiring and training a replacement with no guarantee of success highlight the importance of retaining existing competent employees.

Decreasing turnover begins at the front end, by proper hiring. If a strong sales culture exists, a bank should consider implementing sales aptitude screening tests, and similar measures, to ensure a proper employee fit in a position that includes selling. Several high-performance banks have addressed turnover in the following ways:

- Assigning line managers full responsibility for any staff turnover, determining the cost of turnover, and assigning this cost to the area in which it was incurred.
- Establishing turnover threshold goals with managers and providing them with monthly reports that detail turnover compared to goals.
- Sharing, on a monthly basis, ideas and suggestions that have proven useful in decreasing turnover.

- Identifying high-turnover positions, determining the causes, and then modifying the positions or taking other actions.
- Integrating employee retention goals into manager incentive plans and performance appraisals.

It is crucial that every manager within the bank know exactly what steps to take in the event of a resignation. Table 4–1 itemizes a partial list of action steps with which all managers *must* be familiar.

❏ HANDLING NONPERFORMERS

When instituting a strong sales culture, many bankers whose duties suddenly include selling or sales management do not perform at satisfactory levels. Contrary to popular opinion, a number of banks with high-performance sales cultures have found that termination of employment undermines the building of a sales culture and causes the bank considerable loss, both tangible and intangible.

If a banker has historically performed well but cannot satisfactorily handle new sales responsibilities, termination is the last course of action and should be taken only after all other reasonable means of improving performance are exhausted. In most cases, a bank can improve the sales performance of its employees at a fraction of the cost of hiring and training new employees. For those employees who have consistently been low performers in the past, it is crucial that managers do not use the sales culture as an excuse for termination. If an employee has always performed well but is not doing so in a sales environment, the problem is likely to be an attitudinal (motivational) problem, a lack of specific sales or sales management skills and confidence, or a perception that such a culture change is simply another "here today—gone tomorrow" program.

Managers must deal with nonperformance in a consistent, constructive way:

Table 4–1   Resignation Crisis Action Steps

1. *KEEP THE RESIGNATION QUIET.* As soon as the employee notifies the manager of the intention to resign, the manager should ask the employee to keep the resignation strictly confidential for the next several days (this will eliminate complications in retainment such as employee embarrassment of having "changed my mind" in front of work associates, and rumors that the bank "bought" the employee back).

2. *REACT IMMEDIATELY AND WITH INTENSITY.* Within the next 5 minutes, notify the next manager up in the reporting structure and meet with the employee. If the manager suspects that there is any conflict between him or her and the employee, or that another more senior manager would be of assistance in the retainment attempt, the senior manager should immediately join the discussion. Use all available resources to win. This can mean including the chief executive officer or another senior manager, to emphasize to the employee his or her importance to the organization.

3. *LISTEN CAREFULLY TO THE EMPLOYEE.* It is vital to determine *all* causes that have led the employee to consider resigning. All scheduled meetings or other potential interruptions should be cancelled (retainment of a strong performing employee should take precedence over *any* other business event). Managers must demonstrate by action that the employee is critical to the bank and that the managers consider the relationship a top priority.

4. *CONSTRUCT YOUR ARGUMENTS.* Once all factors that have led the employee to consider resigning have been identified, the managers should then quickly meet (within no more than 10 to 15 minutes) to generate strategies for convincing the employee to remain with the bank. Such strategies should directly address most of the reasons for the resignation and include convincing the employee that the bank offers a total career package that is superior to that offered by the alternative employer (if any).

Table 4–1   (*continued*)

5. *SOLVE THE EMPLOYEE'S PROBLEMS.* If the problems can be corrected, there is a high probability that the employee can be retained. Whether the problems involve job tasks, supervisor conflict, frustration, or other difficulties, they can usually be addressed and corrected. If the employee is not completely convinced, then it is imperative that time be bought by the managers. This will allow the managers to regroup thoughts and schedule another session to attempt to convince the employee to remain. Only two outcomes should result from these meetings: full retainment, or "let's think about this some more and meet to discuss it again in a few . . . ."

6. *WIPE OUT THE COMPETITOR.* If the employee is convinced that the bank offers the best possible career benefits, the managers should then request that the employee contact the other company and flatly refuse the position, leaving no room for additional offers or term modifications.

7. *PREVENT FUTURE PROBLEMS.* Anticipate future problems and work on eliminating them before they develop. Evaluate the employee's specific problems, determine whether they may be applicable to anyone else at the bank, and correct these known problems. This last step should also be the first step in employee retention.

Source: Adaptation from T.J. Rodgers, "No Excuses Management." *Harvard Business Review, 68* (4), July–Aug. 1990: 96–97.

- Enhance the individual's perception and attitude toward sales by encouraging attendance in motivational and esteem-building courses. Often, such courses can be brought into the bank for groups, per request.

- Promptly provide further sales or sales management training to bolster both individual ability and understanding of the sales process and the employee's role.

- Ensure that the sales training received is specific and directly reflects the daily selling situations to which the employees will be exposed to.

- Arrange for the respective employees to meet with their managers again, to mutually set performance goals and objectives that are specific and reachable, yet challenging. Once goals are set, proper sales management follow-up, coaching, and assistance must be provided on a daily and weekly basis.

Most banks find that approximately two-thirds of their original nonperformers begin to sell at satisfactory levels within 3 to 4 months after the training and follow-up steps described. A bank can then focus on the remaining individuals and their managers. If these few remaining employees have performed well in the past, except in the area of sales or sales management, it is likely that they will perform admirably well in other positions that do not involve selling. These individuals will have distinct advantages over new hires in nonsales positions, because they will have a solid knowledge of the bank's operations, procedures, and work channels. As opposed to termination, the bank gains because it can fill a position with an employee of proven operations ability, instead of with a relatively unknown new hire. If these employees are judged on their strengths rather than their weaknesses, the majority will reward the bank with loyalty and performance in areas where they *can* deliver.

❏ MINIMUM PERFORMANCE CRITERIA

Several high-performance banks have established minimum performance threshold criteria for each position (adjusted for market and demographic conditions). If these criteria are not met, a probationary period begins, in which the employee must raise performance to satisfactory levels. If satisfactory sales performance is not met, the employee meets with the Human Resources department and is reassigned to a more suitable non-sales position. The bottom 10 percent of all employees with sales responsibilities is typically targeted for reassignment each year. Minimum performance criteria ensure the systematic removal of unprofitable employees from key retail and wholesale customer contact positions.

❏ ANALYZING NONPERFORMER HIRING

Each time an employee does not perform satisfactorily in a sales position and is either reassigned or terminated, a senior Human Resources manager must meet with the employee's manager to review the employee's past records and identify the reasons why the employee did not work out. The meeting should determine the steps the bank could have taken in its hiring process, training, and work environment, in order to have spotted the problem earlier. The results of such meetings must be directly integrated into the bank's hiring process. Every departure is an opportunity to improve the bank's hiring and retention abilities.

❏ A FINAL TIP

Personnel stability breeds relationships with customers. There are few competitive substitutes for customer relationships.

5

Maximizing Sales Training

Cost-effective and results-oriented sales training will play an increasingly important role in the effectiveness of a sales culture. As banks become more dependent on fee-based and other noninterest income, both product knowledge and sales ability become critical to high performance. The following ideas discussed in the following sections have proven useful in the area of training.

❏ BUILDING AN EDUCATIONAL COMMITTEE

A number of high-performance banks have benefited from establishing an *educational committee*, which meets periodically. The committee typically consists of the chief executive officer, two top executives, senior managers from each department or area, and the training directors or other individuals who have responsibility over the training function. The educational committee is usually separate from the sales leadership committee (discussed in Chapter 2) and typically addresses a broad range of training issues, including sales training. The training director reports directly to this committee and executes the strategies and plans established by the senior executives. The educational committee accomplishes several objectives at once:

- It creates immediate buy-in at the line level because it has visible senior management support.
- It immediately aligns training objectives with the strategies of senior management.
- It ensures proper senior management attention to and involvement in the development of personnel.

Where resources and size allow, some banks have gone a step further and established a bank college. The educational committee typically becomes the board of directors for this college. Topics addressed often include formulating and monitoring the implementation of strategies that will strengthen both a sales and credit culture.

❏ INDIVIDUAL TRAINING PLANS

One of the most important steps in building a sales culture is to perform sales skill assessments of all contact personnel so that specific training topics can be targeted to those individuals who need the training most. The development of individual training plans eliminates the waste of exposing highly experienced relationship managers to basic sales training, yet it identifies specific topics from which the experienced officers would benefit. Its goal is to establish an individual development plan for each employee. An added benefit is its ability to assess bankwide training needs. An example of an individual development plan is shown in Figure 5–1.

❏ SALES CERTIFICATION

Sales certification is a useful tool in creating sales culture uniformity and sales training retention. In some banks, sales certification is necessary for a promotion to a position involving customer contact or to a management position with responsibility for supervising employees who have customer contact. Certification is also frequently used as a criterion for advancement within certain positions. To be certified and to advance to each

Name: _____

Position: _____

Location: _____

Please rank individual based on present skill level (0–5).

Column I: 0—skill *not mastered,* 5—skill *mastered completely.*

Column II: 0—skill *very important* to position, 5—skill *not important* to position.

Column III: Multiply I & II and enter result, lowest scores indicate priority training areas.

SALES SKILLS:	Column I		Column II		Column III
Basic Sales Skills	_____	×	_____	=	_____
Advanced Sales Skills	_____	×	_____	=	_____
Account Management Skills	_____	×	_____	=	_____
Basic Negotiation Skills	_____	×	_____	=	_____
Advanced Negotiation Skills	_____	×	_____	=	_____
Basic Sales Management Skills	_____	×	_____	=	_____
Advanced Sales Management Skills	_____	×	_____	=	_____

PRODUCT KNOWLEDGE:					
Cash Management Products	_____	×	_____	=	_____
Corporate Finance Products	_____	×	_____	=	_____
Credit Products	_____	×	_____	=	_____
Trust Products	_____	×	_____	=	_____

*Lowest scores indicate priority training areas by category.

Figure 5–1 Individual Development Plan (Commercial Officer Example)

new level, an employee must prove competence in specific sales and job skills. Used on both the wholesale and retail sides, certification often involves the following:

- Training attendance and acceptable scores in sales or sales management competencies and product knowledge skills.
- Demonstrated competence in role-playing sessions before senior management, a panel of evaluators, a sales trainer, or the employee's manager.
- Improved on-the-job sales or sales management skills over an established period of time, as observed and signed off by the employee's manager.

❑ REFERRAL CERTIFICATION

To increase bankwide synergy and to maximize sales opportunities, it is essential that all employees be competent at making qualified referrals. A successful method of encouraging this ability is the establishment of *referral certification* by products or departments in such matters as cash management, loan production, trust, private banking, and so on. One leading bank's experiences are detailed as follows:

Our relationship managers, branch managers, and platform representatives are provided with product knowledge training and information in a number of areas and are then asked to demonstrate their referral ability both by written test and by live interviews. The live interviews are done by phone with a product manager or training manager who serves as a referral certifier for each group of products. Successful referral certification in a designated number of areas *and* sales certification result in the awarding of a sales and referral diploma. In addition, we pay cash incentives for each certificate earned and we award a pay-grade increase for earning a sales and referral diploma. Our referral certification program has dramatically increased the ability of our line employees, the number of referrals made, and the additional revenue booked throughout our bank.

❑ JUST-IN-TIME TRAINING DELIVERY

As earnings pressures increase, a number of leading banks have reevaluated existing training delivery formats. Long entry-level programs have been replaced with briefer skills-oriented training at the beginning. Employees are delivered to the line in a shorter period of time and with the precise amount of training necessary to perform their initial job responsibilities. Initial training is interspersed with work periods and rotations, to increase retention of the skills taught and to allow the bank to gain the maximum economic benefit possible, as early as possible. A *just-in-time* (JIT) training delivery format ensures that advanced skills training is delivered just prior to the employee's need. Periodic professional development training is mandatory at all levels and is more targeted, focusing expressly on the skills and tasks each specific employee needs. The result is more efficient use of the bank's training investment.

❑ FORMALIZING ON-THE-JOB TRAINING

Arguably, the most important source of employee skill is on-the-job training. The most cost-effective methods of improving employee skills and capabilities are the targeting and improvement of the on-the-job training process. On-the-job training continues to increase in importance as earnings pressure forces a reduction in the length of traditional training programs within leading banks. High-performance banks can improve their on-the-job training process by taking the following steps:

- Gain commitment to on-the-job training from senior management and all department or branch managers.
- Modify department or branch manager performance appraisals and job descriptions to include specific on-the-job training duties and formal responsibilities.
- Make senior management (or trainers under the direction of senior management) responsible for providing "train-the-trainer" sessions for department and branch managers

to explain the new expectations and to provide useful and specific tools and techniques that can be implemented to accomplish the training objectives.

- Require each department or branch manager to earn new employees by establishing an *on-the-job development plan* for any open position, and to review the plan and tailor it to each new employee.

- Establish a policy that, before promoting or transferring an employee to a new position, managers must develop an on-the-job development plan for that employee and must review the plan with the employee after the position change has been announced.

- Require that department or branch managers place heavy emphasis on effective internal development means, such as rotations, observation, coaching and role playing.

- Include sales, communications, and product knowledge observation and role playing in the on-the-job training of relationship managers and customer-contact employees.

- Evaluate department managers frequently on their implementation, follow-up, and commitment to continuous improvement and development of their employees through on-the-job training.

When a manager does not effectively implement on-the-job development plans, the bank should not transfer or assign new employees to the manager's area until a certain competence and commitment level is reached. A number of banks have expanded on-the-job development plans bankwide, to include those employees who are not new or have not changed positions within a stated time period.

❑ PERFORMANCE APPRAISAL TRAINING OBJECTIVES

It is dangerous to assume that individuals who need sales or other types of training will gain entry into needed training programs on their own. Training needs identified by managers should be noted in every employee's performance appraisal as an objective for the appraisal period. (For an example of training objectives, refer to Figure 3–3.)

❏ TRAINING DELIVERY BY SENIOR MANAGERS

A number of leading banks expect their senior managers to formally train the bank's mid-level officers and relationship managers in key skills. In almost every case, the senior managers have found the training sessions to be the most rewarding and enjoyable days of the entire work year. Senior management involvement will ensure emphasis on the importance of a sales culture and will demonstrate a top-down commitment.

Although it is acceptable for trainers to provide sales management skills training, it is imperative that one of the bank's senior managers deliver the final two parts of a sales management training program in which the bank's sales goals are discussed and specific sales management responsibilities are explained.

❏ DESIGNATING TRAINING AS A COST CENTER

One accountability noticeably absent in most high-performance banks is budget responsibility for training at the department or branch level. When the training area is treated as a profit center rather than a cost center and individual departments or areas are charged back for training, the long-term result is a noticeable decrease in the use of training. Most high-performance banks maintain their training areas as cost centers, despite the short-term attractiveness (especially to the training director) of reverting the training department to a profit center. Maintaining the training area as a cost center ensures strong field participation, senior management commitment, and the ability to implement training strategies quickly. A centralized cost center also eliminates the difficulty of getting budget commitments from every department or area manager throughout the entire bank, in order to put together the resources for a training program.

❑ EVALUATING THE TRAINING SYSTEM

The following criteria are considered important to the success of a well-planned and developed training program:

- Line-driven training that includes involvement in training content, design, and delivery; senior management involvement at both the beginning and end of training delivery, to communicate interest and commitment to both the training process and the success of the individual employees.

- Initial training (for new employees) that is specific, provides the precise skills the employees will need to succeed, establishes a performance level of excellence as the norm of the corporate culture, and emphasizes what makes the bank distinctive from all others.

- Carefully designed on-the-job training that includes planned work assignments, rotations, product knowledge reviews, evaluations, and one-on-one feedback sessions with both the employee's direct manager and the trainers.

- Mandatory professional development training, on a periodic basis, that ensures a high degree of competence in both present and future positions, instills a feeling of progression, and reinforces the importance of training throughout a professional career.

❑ TRAINER AND PROGRAM EVALUATION

It is essential to measure trainer and program impact, to ensure both the progress and the utility of the training. Measurement can be accomplished by the use of participant feedback forms. These forms are often jointly designed by the training manager, who needs feedback from the participants to improve future training; by the senior manager of the areas supported, who needs to verify that the training is on target and covers relevant and needed topics; and by the Human Resources professionals, who need a tool for measuring compensation and advancement.

To properly evaluate the course and trainer, at least two participant evaluations must be completed. The first, typically administered immediately after completion of the course, can provide useful feedback on needed changes in organizational format and on the trainer's delivery skills. The second evaluation, often delivered 3 months after the training program, measures the usefulness and practicality of the skills taught during the course. Basing trainers' rewards, incentives, and promotions on these evaluations ensures that the evaluations will be consistently performed. It is imperative that training effectiveness be measured and improved.

❏ SALES MANAGEMENT TRAINING COMES FIRST

Sales management training does not begin with training line managers; it begins with identifying mid-level and senior managers who are committed to the sales culture. Once identified, these mid-level and senior managers should be taught how to train their line managers and staff. A grave error is the delivery of sales training to selected personnel without first providing sales management training to all relevant management levels. As simple as this point is, many banks either do not consistently train *all* managers or deliver such training only after first providing the training to contact personnel. The result is frustration among the contact personnel because of a perceived lack of sales management support or capability.

❏ SALES MANAGEMENT NEEDS ASSESSMENT

To determine the type of training needed by the bank's sales managers, a confidential questionnaire, to survey the managers' employees, can be implemented. Once the questionnaire is designed, it can be administered to all relationship managers and customer contact personnel. The individual results should be confidential. Access to the survey results should be provided to the relevant department or branch manager who was evaluated, as well as to the training department. The identical survey should be readministered on a quarterly or semiannual basis, and the individual manager should be coached on improvement in each category. A sales management needs assessment is an effective tool for providing an incremental measurement of the sales manager's performance and for fine-tuning individual sales management approaches. A sample sales management needs assessment is illustrated in Figure 5–2.

❏ TRAINING SALES MANAGERS TO SET INDIVIDUAL GOALS

Employee buy-in is critical to proper sales management. Because the buy-in process encourages each individual to share in goal development and to accept the established goals as attainable, each employee has a sense of ownership of the goals and feels that the goals are both reasonable and reachable. Past historical data prove that, when an employee buys-in to a sales or sales management goal, there is a much higher probability that the employee will reach or surpass the goal. All sales management training must include participatory cases that allow each manager the opportunity to practice goal buy-in skills. The importance of buy-in is essential to the sales success of the bank. Sales managers must ensure that the goals finally established are specific, measureable, and controllable by each employee who will be evaluated.

❏ SALES TRAINING CURRICULUM

Many banks find that they need to establish a unique sales training curriculum based on their own markets and competition. Table 5–1 presents a model sales training curriculum that several leading international banks have adapted and used internally. Sales courses are multistaged. The size of the bank and the resources available will limit the extent of the ideal sales training curriculum. The challenge to senior management and the training area is to maximize available resources and to deliver a tailored program that will achieve the bank's sales training goals.

A number of banks have supplemented their basic sales training program by adding one or two days of additional sales role playing after the formal training concludes. This role playing

Name of Manager: _____

Title of Manager: _____

Area/Department: _____

Date: _____

How effective is the sales manager in the following tasks (please choose the most appropriate response from the list below).

a. Extremely effective
b. Very effective
c. Effective
d. Somewhat not effective
e. Not at all effective

1. holding successful sales meetings?

2. providing one-on-one sales coaching?

3. making joint sales calls with employees?

4. providing useful feedback after joint calls?

5. listening to employee needs and problems?

6. responding to employee needs and problems?

Describe the amount of time the manager spends on the following tasks (please choose the most appropriate response from the list below).

a. Far too much time
b. Slightly excessive time
c. Appropriate time
d. Not enough time
e. No time at all

1. holding successful sales meetings?

2. providing one-on-one sales coaching?

3. making joint sales calls with employees?

4. providing useful feedback after joint calls?

5. listening to employee needs and problems?

6. responding to employee needs and problems?

Figure 5–2   Sales Management Perception Survey

7. providing resources and sales support tools?	7. providing resources and sales support tools?
8. supporting sales skills training and practice?	8. supporting sales skills training and practice?
9. asking employees for ideas on improving sales?	9. asking employees for ideas on improving sales?
10. originating ideas on improving sales?	10. originating ideas on improving sales?
11. discussing department/ branch sales goals?	11. discussing department/ branch sales goals?
12. building and motivating a cohesive sales team?	12. building and motivating a cohesive sales team?
13. establishing sales goals jointly with employees?	13. establishing sales goals jointly with employees?
14. supplying or informing on product knowledge?	14. supplying or informing on product knowledge?
15. providing competitive information?	15. providing competitive information?
16. reinforcing the importance of sales?	16. reinforcing the importance of sales?
17. rewarding good performance?	17. rewarding good performance?

Figure 5–2   (continued)

Table 5-1   Model Sales Training Curriculum (Commercial Example)

I.   INITIAL PRODUCT TRAINING (Delivered at entry level).

II. INITIAL SALES TRAINING (Delivered just prior to accompanying experienced lenders to field).

   Basic Sales Training—Provides participants with basic sales skills (i.e., planning a call, opening a call, effective listening, handling objections, closing, selling styles, customer styles, etc.).

III. SALES TRAINING FOR KEY MARKETS (Delivered as appropriate, just prior to assuming a relevant portfolio).

   Selling Small Business Key Products—Focuses on business development and expansion of customer relationships, with emphasis on specific products for small business.

   Selling Middle-Market Key Products—Focuses on business development and expansion of customer relationships, with emphasis on specific products for the middle market.

   Selling Large Corporate Key Products—Centers on business development and expansion of customer relationships, with emphasis on specific products for the large corporate market.

   Selling Private Banking Key Products—Centers on business development and expansion of customer relationships, with emphasis on specific products for the private banking segment.

   Selling Government and Municipalities Key Products—Provides business development skills, with emphasis on specific products for governments and municipalities.

IV. ADVANCED PRODUCT SALES TRAINING (Delivered at 3-month intervals as appropriate to job function).

   Selling Cash Management Products—Provides critical skills necessary to improve effectiveness in selling cash management products.

   Selling Corporate Trust Services—Provides critical skills necessary to improve effectiveness in selling corporate trust services.

Table 5-1 (*continued*)

Selling Corporate Finance Services—Provides critical skills necessary to improve effectiveness in selling sophisticated finance products.

Selling Capital Markets Products—Provides critical skills necessary to improve effectiveness in selling sophisticated capital markets products.

Selling Securities Services—Provides critical skills necessary to improve effectiveness in selling securities services (if applicable).

V. ADVANCED SALES TRAINING (Delivered at 6-month intervals after completion of all product training).

Fee-Income Generation—Focuses on increasing fee-based income and transaction services revenue, by creating new sales opportunities with both existing and new customers.

Advanced Account Management Skills—Provides specific skills in ensuring customer satisfaction and provides strategies to increase revenues generated from each client.

Increasing Account Profitability—Provides relationship managers with specific skills necessary to determine relationship profitability and provides strategies to increase individual customer profitability.

Key Account Management Skills—Focuses on maximizing revenues from key clients by providing skills in identifying and managing relationships with all financial decision makers and influencers.

Sales Presentation Training—Covers setting objectives, analyzing the audience, preparing a written proposal, preparing a verbal presentation, effective delivery, and using visual aids.

Market and Competitive Strategies—Concentrated course on effectively countering and overcoming both direct competitors and general market trends, to ensure maximum relationship profitability.

effectively internalizes the skills learned so that the employees will have both the knowledge and comfort levels necessary to implement the newly gained sales skills on the line.

Because most senior managers realize that initial training is not a cure-all, multistaged sales training programs are becoming common. The initial sales training is usually delivered to new hires, or to all customer contact personnel, when management first implements a transition to a stronger sales culture. This initial training covers the fundamentals of the sales process. The second formal training program is delivered approximately 6 months after the first program and, depending on the audience, often covers advanced account management skills and sales system development. This secondary training may dissect certain portions of the sales process, using case study formats and suggesting strategic sales planning skills. Additional sales training, often held on a bi-yearly basis, is structured around case studies and role plays dealing with real account manager or customer contact situations. An acceptance of continuing education and of training in sales skills throughout a career in banking is vital to developing these skills in each employee.

❏ STAGING TELLER SALES TRAINING

Tellers receive little sales training because of their high turnover ratios. The training is frequently limited to a day or less in a 1- or 2-week training program. Although brief initial sales training might be realistic in the short run, many banks have begun to offer in-depth sales training, after 6 months of employment, to those tellers who remain. In a few of these banks, the sales training is mandatory before the teller can be promoted to a higher position or pay level. This strategy ensures both cost-effective initial teller training and superior sales training when the bank can recoup its additional investment.

❏ CROSS-DEPARTMENTAL TRAINING

A way in which some banks have successfully increased both teamwork and product knowledge is by introducing cross-departmental training. During departmental or branch sales meetings, a guest representative from another department is brought in to deliver a 5- to 15-minute presentation. This briefing provides information on products that are most relevant to the audience, how those products work, how they can benefit the customer, what customer profile to look for, how to make a referral, and the names of important contacts for referral purposes. A key to the success of such programs is for the speaker to provide brief, written, product and contact summaries for the audience. Binders are often provided to each employee, for collecting and organizing the summaries. On the retail side, where there may possibly be too many branches to make visitations cost-effective, banks provide their branch managers with overviews and product profiles at meetings, for later discussion. When the branch managers return to their branches, they then deliver the information at their sales meetings.

❏ BRANCH MANAGER REFERRAL TRAINING

To effectively develop branch managers who can make proper referrals to commercial, trust, and private banking departments, banks often establish sales training follow-up classes, to provide branch managers with a basic understanding of commercial lending products, institutional trust products, and so on. A description of one such program in a top performing bank follows:

> As in most banks, our branch managers felt very uncomfortable in qualifying prospects and then making referrals to other parts of the bank. They were not confident because they lacked product knowledge, were inexperienced in selling the relevant products, and lacked a good contact name in each department, to be passed along to the prospect. To correct this situation, we designed a branch manager referral training program, delivered partly as a correspondence course with testing, and partly as a classroom course. The correspondence portion of the program increased product knowledge, while the classroom portion allowed branch

managers to meet managers of other departments and to become more comfortable with selling other products through extensive practice sessions and role playing. The training has enabled our branch managers to identify opportunities, screen leads, and facilitate the referral process. The program has been very well received and has tangibly increased the number of referrals, ultimately leading to profitable bank customers.

❑ COMMERCIAL FEE-BASED INCOME TRAINING

As noninterest income becomes a greater component of a bank's total revenues, relationship managers realize that lending is only one of many services they need to understand and discuss with their customers. A strong knowledge of basic services such as cash management products should be viewed as critical to the job function. Fee-based income and transactional services revenue provide the key to increased margins and profitability in a competitive environment where traditional lending often involves the assumption of increased risk to maintain market share. Commercial relationship managers must be trained to expect profit from every relationship, even if, as with referral fees for private placements, the business is not bankable. Creativity and improved relationship manager abilities can conquer existing views of limited job functions, allowing a bank's wholesale area to differentiate itself and outperform competitors.

Banks must develop comprehensive programs to ensure competence by both new and experienced employees. This trend is highly evident in wholesale banking: each year, relationship managers are becoming more dependent on fees from cash management products, private placements, corporate finance activities, expanded trust and custodial products, and mezzanine financing. Relationship managers must be trained so that they are able to sit down with their customers and explain all the capabilities that their respective bank can bring forth directly or through intermediaries. Value-added consulting and product knowledge are key skills that lead to customer loyalty in an advanced sales culture.

❑ SALES PERCEPTION TRAINING

Most entry-level sales training programs focus on training skills in the selling process. Unfortunately, these programs often do not spend enough time focusing on why a banker should sell. Most bankers do not initially envision selling as part of their job responsibilities. Many have a very negative view of sales, which must be addressed in all initial sales training programs.

Some relationship managers feel that sales calls are an inconvenience and a disturbance to their business customers. Research has proven, however, that local businessmen feel great pride in meeting their present or potential bankers. They appreciate the attention and think highly of the banker for taking the time to meet with them. Once a relationship manager realizes that a sales call is not demeaning but, instead, benefits the banker's image and respectability, the relationship manager will be much more apt to perform regular customer and prospect visits. Branch managers must also be trained to think positively about selling. Customers welcome advice and assistance in making financial decisions, especially if this assistance comes from someone they trust and value: their banker.

❑ INITIAL TEAM-BUILDING TRAINING

Lack of communication and referrals between departments is frequently traceable to the absence of friendships and bonds among employees from all areas of the bank. Yet, new retail and wholesale employees are typically trained separately, because of the vastly different credit and operational skills needed by each group. This segregation often widens the border between various departments; consequently, many teamwork and referral opportunities are lost throughout these bankers' careers.

Several banks have found that, if the initial 3 to 4 weeks of training is performed jointly, bonds form between the two groups that will last throughout their careers at the institution. Teamwork and referral levels between the retail and wholesale sides in banks that use joint initial training are often substantially higher than in those banks that do not.

❑ PRODUCT-OF-THE-MONTH TRAINING

One way to successfully increase product knowledge is to name a product-of-the-month during each sales meeting. Profiles of this product are distributed and reviewed during the sales meeting. They can be accompanied by a special promotion on the product or increased incentive pay for selling it during that month.

❑ PRODUCT FOCUS SESSIONS

Several banks hold focus sessions in which product managers or specialists meet with the bank's relationship managers. In these 1-day focus sessions, product profiles or fact sheets are distributed to the relationship managers. They then team up and practice role playing in small groups in which product specialists or product managers provide feedback. The relationship managers are often required to bring a list of clients who would be most suitable for each product. Meeting with the product managers or specialists provides the relationship managers with an opportunity to ask direct questions and to determine the best way to approach each client. An action plan is then developed for each client, for follow-up by the relationship managers during the following week. Some banks even set short-term product sales goals after each product focus session.

❑ PRODUCT KNOWLEDGE GAMES

One effective method of increasing product knowledge is to develop a card game. Question and answer cards, with various degrees of difficulty, are prepared on relevant banking products. The cards are then divided into three stacks: least, moderately, and most challenging. There should be at least 60 cards per stack. A fourth stack should be of red cards and a fifth, of green cards. Two or more people divide the question cards and quiz each other in a round-robin fashion. Each correct answer earns a green card, worth 1 point, and each incorrect answer earns a red card, which costs a 2-point deduction. The person with the highest score wins. Because the stacks are of different difficulty levels, a relatively new person could play against a senior person and still present a challenge. As product knowledge is absorbed, employees progressively move up to more challenging stacks until they have mastered the entire set. This competitive game is fun, but, most importantly, it is addictive and is often played during lunch breaks.

A number of banks have set up product knowledge contests similar to television game shows; various departments and branches send teams to compete against one another. On the retail side, some banks have had interbranch competitions leading to championship matches once or twice per year. Regardless of the method used, games can serve as a highly effective medium to ensure both the exposure and retention of product knowledge.

❏ INTERNALIZING SKILLS

Traditional training usually involves attending a seminar, listening to lectures or presentations, reading material, or watching videos. After returning from the seminar, the average participant catches up with backlogged work, returns the stacked-up phone messages, contains any fires that have cropped up, and then tries to recall and use skills taught in the training session (which seem to become more distant in time, as each week goes by). One leading bank has modified its traditional training delivery system in this way:

> Effective training involves internalizing skills. Our training is now delivered close to the employee's workplace and the employee's work schedule is not interrupted. The training classes meet once per week over a period of time. Each participant reads the material, takes part in role plays, and tries the new skills the next day on the line. Did it work? Each participant speaks to the instructor and other participants at the next class session. After some coaching and comparison of notes, the new skills are tried again, again, and again. The practice, role playing, and modeling are based on real situations. Lecturing and content breaks are short, compressed, and practiced immediately after the lecture is over. Feedback by

observers and assessors is provided consistently, immediately following each simulation or role play. The participants modify and adapt the new skills to work in their particular environment and situation. Only in this manner can the skills become internalized and effective in daily work situations.

Although the delivery of training in this manner might be logistically challenging, the magnitude of the improvement in retention and internalization of skills makes this delivery method attractive.

❏ EMPLOYEES AS CUSTOMERS

Studies have shown that an employee must have empathy for a customer. To help increase both empathy and awareness of quality service, several banks require new employees to shop their own bank as customers, as part of their initial training. Some banks have even integrated shopping the competitors' offices and services into their training curriculum. After the shopping is done, the participants are brought together for a roundtable discussion. All aspects of the experience are examined from a customer's perspective.

❏ LUNCH SPEAKER SESSIONS

Several banks have implemented *Lunch-n-Learn* sessions at their corporate or main offices. These Lunch-n-Learn meetings typically last less than an hour. Interested employees bring sack lunches to a meeting room where a speaker (who may be an internal or external resource) delivers a training presentation (often directed at personal or professional growth). In almost every instance, these monthly or weekly programs have had great success. Turnout is typically far higher than expected, and senior officers frequently attend, to hear the speaker and to mix with people from other departments and areas. All that is needed to launch these sessions is a vacant meeting room during lunch hour, a speaker, a topic, and flyers to distribute throughout the building and nearby offices, announcing the session.

❑ ESTABLISHING TRAINEE JOB DESCRIPTIONS

Several banks develop job descriptions specifically for new employees who are in training. The job descriptions state the objectives of the training, the performance criteria, and the acceptable performance levels. In addition to helping the trainees to understand their responsibilities during the initial training period, the trainee job descriptions justify the termination of those trainees who do not perform to expectations during the training period.

❑ ACCESS TO PERFORMANCE APPRAISALS

Both management and the training area should have access to averaged, overall results of bankwide performance appraisals grouped by department, function, and branch. To avoid unnecessary disclosure, performance appraisal results should be tabulated and averaged by departments or areas; individual performance results are confidential. The results should be organized by topic areas, competencies, and skills, to assist management in pinpointing problem areas. Conveying performance appraisal results is necessary to modify training and management techniques. Weak areas or skills can then be addressed.

❑ INTERNAL OR EXTERNAL TRAINING

In determining whether to use internal or external sales training programs and personnel, managers should first define the bank's training objectives and then examine available internal resources. By answering several questions, the choice will become clear:

- Does the bank have strong internal trainers or mid-level managers who are willing to deliver advanced sales and sales management training to branch and regional managers, commercial and trust officers and other personnel?
- Does the bank presently have, or can it quickly develop, a strong sales and sales management training program that

can be customized to meet the specialized needs of each of the different departments or areas?

- What budget allocations exist or could be approved for funding the necessary training within the bank?

- What credibility issues might an inside trainer face (versus an external consulting firm)?

- Is it cost-effective to develop an internal training program and maintain the overhead of skilled sales and sales management trainers (versus an outside program)?

- Is it cost-effective to pay an outside firm licensing fees per participant, as well as developmental and delivery fees, in applications with large audiences? Would internal design and delivery be more cost-effective?

- Can the outside firm customize the program to incorporate the bank's specific products and competitive environment, and can it provide training on sales tracking forms, corporate strategies, and other specific concepts essential to building the bank's sales culture?

❏ FINDING SALES TRAINERS AND DEVELOPERS

Many sources of talent are available to develop and deliver exceptional internal sales programs. High-performing internal producers are often made sales trainers for 12 to 18 months as a rotational intermediary step between the line and management. Another good source materializes when sales trainers and developers are hired away from vendors who provide sales and sales management training. What better way to fill a position than to find a training professional within the banking arena who already designs and delivers sales training on a daily basis? A manager who is unsure of what firms to contact should obtain vendor lists published annually in trade publications and periodicals. Other excellent sources include trainer associations, and candidates from competitor and noncompetitor banks. Finding the right individuals to deliver training is essential to the success of the sales culture, because these individuals will be in highly visible positions—both while delivering training and in support roles.

❏ NEGOTIATING WITH TRAINING VENDORS

It is important for a bank to stress to an outside training firm that pricing will be an important consideration and that they will be competing with at least two other vendors for the assignment. Most firms price according to what they think the bank will pay and how competitive they feel they must be. It is essential to adjust the vendors' thinking to the lowest possible pricing *before* a proposal is delivered, regardless of how large the training budget may be. After the bank has narrowed its search and verified references, the relevant firms should be notified that they are final contenders and asked whether any flexibility in the pricing is possible. A lower price would incline the bank toward choosing that company for the business. Any savings (over estimate) will allow the bank to provide additional training or customizing while still meeting budget constraints.

A manager should never request more than one conciliation at a time, and should be firm regarding the terms. Contact with the firms should be made early, so that the bank can appear to delay its decision; time is a primary negotiating tool for the bank. When pricing is agreed on, the outside firm should be approached on other issues such as whether the bank's internal trainers can observe the training at no charge. When all details have been finalized, everything should be documented.

If the consulting firm will be delivering the training or designing a customized program, managers should be aware that most firms have several different program developers and trainers, and each has different abilities and areas of specialization. Before discussing pricing, the manager should ask for the names and backgrounds of the company's *top* trainers and curriculum designers, and insist on meeting these individuals where possible. If trainers and developers are not selected before pricing is negotiated, the training company will often assign its lowest-cost (and often, least capable) specialists to design and deliver the training.

❏ LIFETIME TRAINING CONCEPT

One way in which top banks have differentiated their employee development efforts is by establishing a lifetime training concept. Impossible to accomplish without strong senior management commitment, lifetime training focuses on the continuing educational process after entry-level training. Most banks that use this system establish an entire curriculum of courses, both internal and external, for the bank's officers and other employees. Two training sessions per year are often mandatory, and this goal is defined and evaluated in each officer's performance appraisal. Mandatory training session topics can be decided by both the employees and their managers before each new performance period, based on individual strengths and weaknesses. For relationship managers, typical courses include one technical or credit course and one sales-oriented course on key account management, advanced sales skills, advanced sales management, account management, team building, or maximizing strategic markets.

This long-term commitment to training is most evident in banks that have strong management and earnings stability. In many of these high-performance banks, both senior and mid-level managers have endorsed the lifetime training process and may deliver portions of the training themselves.

❏ GOAL SETTING AFTER TRAINING

Immediately after sales or sales management training is delivered, the participants and their managers, along with the sales support manager (if any), should meet to jointly establish new sales goals for each participant. The time gap between the end of the training and the meeting should be no longer than a week (ideally, it should be held the following business day). Establishing new goals immediately after sales training reinforces selling skill retention and bolsters the participant's performance expectations and target goals.

❑ SALES MANAGEMENT POST-TRAINING BRIEFING

Total sales management training delivery consists of three distinct parts, the last two of which are often missing in average-performance banks:

1. Traditional delivery of general or advanced sales management techniques;
2. Review of the bank's overall and specific sales goals and strategies, and of how each participant plays an integral role in helping the bank reach its sales goals.
3. Definition of each manager's specific responsibilities and the actual training of the managers to effectively use the bank's sales tracking tools to monitor progress toward the established goals.

The second and third parts of the overall sales management training process should always be delivered by a senior manager, to emphasize the importance of sales management and to ensure that the bank's goals and strategies are properly relayed.

❑ THE IMPACT OF FOLLOW-UP ON RESULTS

The importance of training follow-up is critical. Banks that track performance after training realize that performance levels initially increase for 3 to 5 months and then decrease again, unless there is follow-up. When follow-up is provided after training, performance continues to improve and ultimately achieves a higher level than was reached immediately after training. Training creates new skills but only practice and reinforcement result in skills internalization and use on the job.

6

Enhancing Sales Aids and Tools

Maximizing sales effectiveness involves providing customer contact employees with the right tools and sales aids. These tools and aids can increase bank margins by improving cross-sell ratios, justifying value-added services, or providing a means to differentiate the bank from its competitors, in order to win new customers and retain existing ones. Each of the following concepts is used by one or more leading banks, with proven results.

☐ RED CARPET COURTESY

Several banks have replaced their traditional teller-line "cattle rails" for a winding, plush, red carpet that traces the original teller-line path. Instead of following the dehumanizing rails used by most banks, customers simply follow the carpet, a symbol of respect for the customer as a person. Banks that use carpet lines report no trouble with line cutting and they find that the carpet provides a highly effective means of differentiating the bank over its competitors. Red carpet courtesy is frequently coupled with advertising that promotes a more humane treatment of customers.

111

❏ IN-BRANCH CUSTOMER SERVICE PHONES

One way to increase selling time in a branch is to move out nonsales, labor-intensive tasks. A successful method of accomplishing this is to place direct-dial customer service phones next to the waiting area at each branch. These phones are typically made semiprivate by use of smoked glass partitions, plants, or other means. The phones increase service because customers have an alternative to platform representatives, who are often tied up with other customers. Any customers who desire personal attention over quick service will tend to wait for a service representative to become available. The bank can then service all customers better by:

- Providing faster service to those who desire personal attention.
- Providing immediate service via phone to those who prefer quick answers and would be inconvenienced by waiting for a service representative's assistance.
- Increasing the time a service representative can spend with both new and existing customers, and allowing more time to cross-sell. Having fewer time constraints also leads to service levels superior to those the competition can offer, and at a lower cost.

❏ ESTABLISHING A KEY CUSTOMER PROGRAM

In most banks, the top 1 to 2 percent of all retail bank customers account for 15 to 25 percent of all bank deposits. Because low costs-of-funds are vital to overall profitability, it is essential to retain large depositors. Furthermore, 20 to 30 percent of all customers account for 70 to 80 percent of all profits in most banks. Many high-performance banks attract and retain top customers by establishing *key customer programs.*

A key customer program focuses an escalating amount of attention on the bank's top 20, 10, 5, 1, and 0.5 percent of wholesale and retail customers, preferably in terms of profitability. The program provides a system of greater rewards and attention, depending on each customer's ranking. The increased focus ranges from newsletters and speaker lunches, for the top 20 percent, to event tickets and lunches with the president and senior officers, for the top 0.5 percent. Assignment of a personal banking officer to each customer has also been a successful step. A common benefit offered to key customers is the ability to reach their personal banker 24 hours a day, by means of a message center. There should be a service guarantee that all customer messages are personally returned on the same day. Other special services, such as birthday cards and invitations to selected functions, create strong bank loyalty. A sound plan should include the following goals:

- Lower the bank's cost-of-funds by retaining and increasing low-cost deposits.
- Increase deposit stability by increasing customer loyalty.
- Avoid attracting or retaining deposits by paying high rates.
- Provide additional services by maximizing use of already reduced overhead.
- Increase fee-income by top customer usage of additional bank services.

It is both easier and more cost-effective to sell additional bank services to satisfied and profitable customers than to nonprofitable customers with fewer relationships. It is even more costly to acquire noncustomers and convert them into profitable bank relationships. The bank's existing base of profitable customers offers the best source of increased future revenue.

❏ VIP DINNERS

Often planned for a select portion of a bank's top business and personal customers, these dinners feature heavy senior officer representation and an interesting keynote speaker after the dinner. Banks frequently invite the top 5 to 10 percent of their business customers and the top 1 to 2 percent of their retail customers, based on relationship profitability or deposit and loan activity. These dinners are held on a regional basis, and customers are invited two to four times per year.

❏ CONSOLIDATED CUSTOMER STATEMENTS

In reviewing the total package of customer services, one of the most visible and tangible offerings is the monthly customer statement. Improving the design of the statement provides a bank with an opportunity to differentiate its services from those of competitors. By designing consolidated statements that detail all account relationships on one report, banks can provide a much better view of the customer's total financial position. A consolidated statement offers an incentive to shift all banking relationships to a single institution.

The system should also be sophisticated enough to provide marketing messages in those areas where the customer does not use the bank. Many systems scan all customer accounts and perform a rudimentary analysis. For example, if a customer has high balances in time deposits but does not have a retirement account with the bank, there is a probability that this customer has a retirement account at another institution. Thus, a message would appear in the customer's consolidated statement promoting the bank's retirement account and listing incentives for the customer to open a new account or to roll over an existing account away from the competing institution.

The structure of a customer statement usually flows from general to specific, and uses a similar format to display information on each product. Enhanced graphics, better fonts, and increased personalization make this statement a valuable and easily understood tool for bank customers. The first page of a consolidated statement typically summarizes all relationships with the bank, including balances of checking accounts, money market accounts, retirement accounts, savings, installment loans, mortgage loans, credit lines, time deposit balances, and even time deposit renewal reminders. The integrated sales and promotional messages also make consolidated statements valuable as sales tools.

❏ FINANCIAL PLANNING SEMINARS

An effective retail tool that has long been underutilized is financial planning seminars. These seminars build strong relationships with existing customers and attract preferred customers from other banks. Although bankers sometimes fear that providing financial counseling will lead to outflows of core deposits into higher return instruments (intermediation), virtually every bank that has instituted financial planning seminars reports the opposite result: increased confidence and business between the customer and the bank.

Financial planning seminars are usually held on weekday nights or Saturdays. Seminars are announced in mailings to prospective or selected existing clients. Marketing databases or relationship management systems vastly simplify announcements. The mailings usually provide a telephone number or a return envelope, to confirm attendance. The seminars are usually conducted by a regional manager or exceptional branch manager within the proximate geographic mailing area. They are usually held once each quarter and provide an excellent opportunity to differentiate a bank's level of service from others in a competitive market. Frequent topics for financial planning seminars include educational financing, home-buying advice, and retirement planning. The seminars often conclude with the setting of individual appointments with customers, to expand the banking relationship.

❏ AFFINITY GROUP FINANCIAL ROUNDTABLES

An extremely successful value-added service, financial roundtables create strong wholesale customer loyalty and unique opportunities to gain new customers. The roundtables are organized by a bank officer who contacts the senior financial officers of major local corporations and invites them to half-day sessions on a quarterly basis. The site can be a vacant bank boardroom, or the bank can ask the financial officers to volunteer meeting space on a rotational basis. Topics for discussion are solicited before the meeting, placed on a flip chart, and covered during the meeting. The bank officer's duty is to serve as a moderator and to plan and invite participants to upcoming meetings. General financial roundtables have been so successful that some banks also host industry-specific affinity group financial roundtables (depending on the depth of the client base in specific industries) or roundtables segmented by company revenues. In addition to pleasing existing customers by affording them an opportunity to associate with their peers, the bank gains valuable credibility and exposure to senior financial officers of prospective firms.

❏ SMALL-BUSINESS ASSISTANCE PROGRAMS

A tool used successfully to increase emerging middle-market revenues is a small-business assistance program which, through seminars, helps high-potential, small-business owners with cash management guidance and other bank services. This assistance creates bank loyalty, increases the chances of success for the business, and provides the bank's officers with further insight into a business and its managers, before the bank loans out money or incurs other risks.

Some banks also schedule branch seminars run by small-business relationship managers. This service allows hesitant borrowers to meet with a small-business relationship manager before requesting a loan. During the seminar, small-business owners are briefed on the bank's lending policies and requirements, which gives the potential borrower an opportunity to ask questions and seek advice in a nonthreatening environment, without fear of loan rejection. Small-business programs tend to build strong relationships and loyalties.

❏ YOUNG CONSUMER ORIENTATION

The young adult market can be reached with young consumer orientations in which the bank teams up with local high schools to provide seniors with instructional programs on banking. The primary goals of the bank are to boost its image, develop new accounts, and sell such young adult products as student loans. Young consumer orientations make an excellent contribution toward outperforming other banks in market share over the long term.

❏ CORPORATE VIP CLUBS

Several banks have established clubs for top corporate executives. They qualify, yearly or semiyearly, based on relationship profitability quantified by their company's average balances, outstandings, or other factors. Membership benefits include access to conference rooms, private phone booths, receptionist/ secretarial services, facsimile and mail services, message service, tended bar and snack service, and, in some cases, access to personal computers and physical recreation equipment. Usually located in a bank's key downtown market areas, often in the bank's own building or contracted through a local health or luncheon club, corporate VIP clubs increase customer loyalty and provide relationship managers with a highly effective sales tool. These same corporate VIP clubs can be made available to small-business customers and top retail customers for an additional tiered fee based on deposits or other usage or monthly criteria. Small-business and top retail customers are frequently allowed to pay for yearly enrollment in the club by using soft dollars awarded to them on their monthly statements, based on relationship profitability.

❏ BRANCH REDESIGN

Although many branch marketing aids marginally improve retail sales, the redesign of the retail branch floor has led to significant improvement for some banks. By assigning more branch floor space to platform personnel and relationship managers, often at the expense of the teller area, and by building individually enclosed offices with conspicuous customer signage, many retail facilities have improved sales performance. Insurance, travel, brokerage, and nontraditional investment personnel may also be given individual offices with signage. In high-volume offices, the effectiveness of this strategy can be further enhanced by adding a trained receptionist to direct traffic and provide preliminary marketing information, should customers need to wait.

Visual point-of-purchase (POP) marketing tools can often stimulate demand and increase the effectiveness of a sales culture. Intangible products such as loans can often be turned into tangible ones with photographic enlargements of boats, new cars, and vacation homes. Enhancing product descriptions with visuals improves the sales value of brochures. POP signs should be life-size, illuminated, and easily visible from customer waiting areas. Because the whole purpose of POPs is to increase margins with a relatively weak marketing tool, POPs must be obtained and installed at a low cost or they will negatively impact branch profitability. Full advantage should be taken of both seasonal and impulse products, in choosing products to feature.

❑ IMPROVING BRANCH RATE SIGNS

A lobby sign listing depository products is a tradition for virtually all banks. It is highly useful in reminding customers, on a continual basis, about the availability of such products. A number of banks have challenged the idea of posting interest rates next to each product. By referring customers to platform representatives for rates, several banks have been able to increase both margins and volume of products sold. The platform representatives will typically have daily deposit price sheets, which they can personalize with the potential depositor's name and review in light of the customer's individual needs. Personalized and dated rate sheets can serve as reminders and incentives for customers to return, should a sale not be made immediately. Rate sheets are usually printed on high-quality paper and distributed to the branches the day before rate changes take effect. In heavily automated branches, they are printed on-site.

Most banks that have tried using a time deposit sign without rates during a 6-month trial period have implemented the change permanently. With a well trained staff, personalized rate sheets for customers can decrease a bank's fund costs while increasing customer loyalty. When should rates be posted or quoted over the phone and in lobbies? When the particular bank pays one of the highest rates in the market and is willing to continue paying a premium for deposits. This is not a high-performance strategy!

❏ TELLER REFERRAL BADGES

Teller referral badges have long been effective in achieving referrals, but are most bank tellers wearing badges at this very moment? The likelihood is that they are not. A policy should be established to encourage tellers to wear referral badges at all times. To increase the effectiveness of the badges and to rotate among different featured products, banks frequently purchase reusable pin-on badges into which the featured product insert can be slid. The referral badge promotion is usually changed bi-weekly or monthly. The Marketing Department is in charge of choosing the new referral products and printing the referral badge inserts. Most banks with highly developed sales cultures ensure that their tellers wear referral badges every day, not just during special promotional efforts.

❏ MOTIVATIONAL EMPLOYEE MAIL

This tool is highly effective in motivating all bank employees who have sales responsibilities. Motivational employee mail is often used in conjunction with special promotionals or year-end bonuses and prizes. One bank does it this way:

> The bank decided to send its top sales performers and their spouses to a tropical island in lieu of bonuses, cash prizes, and other awards. The contest was announced at the beginning of the year and six mailings were planned, one every other month. These were sent directly to the home of each employee with sales responsibilities. One mailing consisted of a brochure from the island, showing the beaches and the extravagant accommodations. Another consisted of a miniature zip-lock bag with a small amount of white

sand, a sea shell, and a picture postcard of the island. Another mailing consisted of shirts imprinted with the island's name. The effectiveness of the motivational mailings on the employees (*and their spouses*) was remarkable. The contest was an overwhelming success, providing motivation throughout the entire year.

Other banks focus their motivational mail or catalog gifts and other prizes for which the employees can qualify. The various possibilities and uses of employee motivational mail are endless and can be extremely effective in building a high-performance sales culture.

❑ PERSONALIZED LETTERS TO CUSTOMERS

As a variant from most direct mail or customer newsletters, several banks send monthly or bi-monthly personalized letters, highly customized, from each department or branch head to their respective customers. These personalized letters highlight recent activity of the department or branch and provide an overview of its different key products or services. The personalized letters have the appearance of being hand-typed and signed by the respective branch or department manager. By keeping customers up-to-date on events and people they know, customer relationships are strengthened. These mailings can be done with little more than a database and word processor. Larger banks centralize the process but still provide customized letters written by the managers of the departments or branches that serve the customers.

Although customer letters signed by the president or chief executive officer are far better than nothing, most intuitive bankers realize that a main objective of customer mailings is to build stronger relationships with the customer and that these relationships are built on the line between customers and the bank's employees who deal with them regularly. Thus, marketing efforts that promote line relationships are usually more effective than those that attempt to establish a relationship with an officer whom the customer might meet once a year, if at all.

☐ SALES TRACKING TOOLS

The industry has seen a large influx of software and hardware packages that support sales tracking and incentive management. Most banks prefer to buy their software for faster implementation of time, avoidance of an unknown product developed internally, and utilization of outside expertise that often comes with the purchase of a system. When an incentive plan is implemented to increase bank profitability, a fundamental issue is the expense and method of tracking. If considering a tracking system by an outside provider, the bank must determine what it would like tracked, before choosing a package. All too often, a bank chooses a system before deciding on the variables it would like to track. The bank is then forced to let the system dictate what will or will not be tracked.

☐ DEVELOPING RELATIONSHIP MANAGEMENT DATABASES

The marketing area should provide each relationship manager and branch manager with direct support, by means of an individual relationship management database. This database is usually in the form of a monthly report that lists all customers and prospects in the officer's assigned area. The report should be compressed to a size that is portable for each officer at all times, and it should be detailed enough to provide relevant information and contact names for each prospective customer. In turn, the relationship manager or branch manager should be responsible for providing the marketing area with monthly list changes and updates.

Several banks have experimented with automated weekly listings of local businesses, prospects, and customers who should be contacted. Providing and centrally updating such lists reduces the amount of time relationship managers need to spend on generating the lists themselves. The building of individual relationship manager databases also ensures solid and thorough coverage of all territories or regions, clearly defines what is expected of individual officers, and reduces information loss due to turnover and transfers.

A number of banks use relationship management systems that track customers and prospects by company name, decision makers, influencers, applicable products, existing or potential revenue amount, and the probability of securing revenue. More powerful systems provide automated reporting features such as customer rankings by potential profitability. This reporting helps relationship managers to select and focus on high-potential customers and prospects.

❏ RELATIONSHIP MANAGEMENT DATABASE EVALUATION

The primary goal of most relationship management database systems is to provide a comprehensive source of customer and relationship information that can be effectively used to increase sales and service. Top relationship management systems then assist relationship managers in identifying additional bank products for customer use. The most cost-effective utilization of relationship management automation systems is in wholesale banking and high-end retail applications, where specific branches cater to customers with legitimate needs for additional bank products and services. Highly effective but still controversial is the extreme branch automation several high-performance banks have embarked on in their upper-end markets, in order to maximize the return on their investment in automation. A traditional systemwide blanket strategy is the basis for comparison. Criteria frequently considered when evaluating relationship management systems are provided in Table 6–1.

❏ PRODUCT KNOWLEDGE LEARNING SYSTEMS

As retail automation increases, several high-performance retail banks use software systems that test relationship managers and platform representatives on both product knowledge and sales techniques. These automated tutorial and testing sessions are

Table 6–1   Relationship Management System Evaluation—Basic
Checklist

Sales Tools

_____ Suggest prospective services needed, based on *all* accounts, balances, age, etc.?

_____ Intuitively provide sales scripts and graphic images, to assist in cross-selling services?

Training Tools

_____ Built-in product knowledge tutorial, to minimize necessary "in-classroom" training?

_____ Built-in tests that challenge employee retention of new product information?

_____ Automatic comparison, scoring, and reporting of above game against peer employees?

Marketing Tools

_____ Allow relationship managers to keep databases of high-potential prospects?

_____ Find market share, average accounts per household, and other information, by zip code or other segment?

_____ Compare present results to past-period results, and provide trend analysis?

_____ Identify high-value customers, based on deposit sizes or other criteria?

Profitability

_____ Determine profitability by customer relationship, product, department, and employee?

_____ Provide profitability and market share projections, based on pricing variables by product?

_____ Speed up account opening and maintenance tasks, to allow more selling time?

Table 6–1 (*continued*)

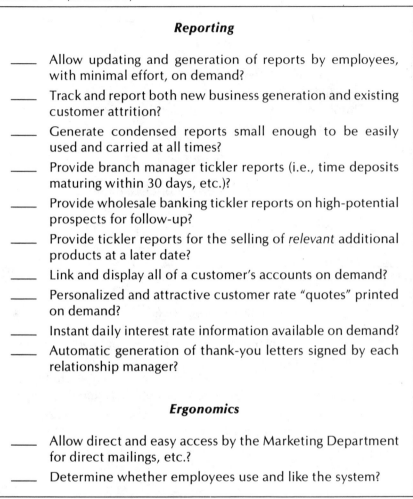

Reporting

_____ Allow updating and generation of reports by employees, with minimal effort, on demand?

_____ Track and report both new business generation and existing customer attrition?

_____ Generate condensed reports small enough to be easily used and carried at all times?

_____ Provide branch manager tickler reports (i.e., time deposits maturing within 30 days, etc.)?

_____ Provide wholesale banking tickler reports on high-potential prospects for follow-up?

_____ Provide tickler reports for the selling of *relevant* additional products at a later date?

_____ Link and display all of a customer's accounts on demand?

_____ Personalized and attractive customer rate "quotes" printed on demand?

_____ Instant daily interest rate information available on demand?

_____ Automatic generation of thank-you letters signed by each relationship manager?

Ergonomics

_____ Allow direct and easy access by the Marketing Department for direct mailings, etc.?

_____ Determine whether employees use and like the system?

scored and compared with results from other peer employees. Banks with such capabilities require their employees to review a certain amount of "course work" each month and to take the accompanying quizzes during slow periods or down time. These automated learning systems not only ensure that all relevant officers and platform representatives are familiar with existing products, but that new products will be successfully launched by creating systemwide competence on minimal notice. It is crucial for a bank's own staff to be able to post product knowledge material and quizzes to the system. Contests and incentives are often partially based on success at mastering the product knowledge questions in the system. One bank's experience is described below:

> Once the automated product knowledge system was implemented, a number of branch, regional, and bankwide contests were held, based on individual scores by product areas. Product knowledge increased dramatically with each passing month as more product areas were mastered. Sales, especially for lucrative nontraditional products, improved dramatically as a direct result of the program. For the first time, *most* relationship managers and platform representatives felt comfortable discussing and selling complex products and services that only our superstars would sell before. Best of all, the product knowledge and sales skills were learned during slow periods, when little productive work would otherwise have resulted. Continual product knowledge improvement is now the norm for experienced employees, and new employees become profitable in a much shorter time period than before the system was implemented.

❏ BUILDING CUSTOMER MARKETING PROFILES

What better way to increase the effectiveness of a bank's wholesale and retail marketing efforts than by basing these efforts on information acquired from individual customers at account opening? When first meeting with customers, a well-trained relationship manager or platform representative identifies a number of appropriate services and then tries to cross-sell as many of these services as possible. Services that are not cross-sold immediately represent future opportunities.

A *customer marketing profile* is a form or screen that allows the bank employee to document potential opportunities for future follow-up by direct mail, telemarketing, or other means. This form, designed by the Marketing Department, contains a list of all relevant bank products, as well as space for comments. A bank can make the submission of customer marketing profiles mandatory for all customers or can promote usage by awarding points or other incentives to contacting employees.

7

Better Feedback and Communication

Providing the line with competitive intelligence, performance data, information on upcoming incentives and promotions, referral contacts, and praise depends on a well-developed communication system.

☐ PERFORMANCE FEEDBACK REPORTS

Feedback is crucial to the development of a high-performance sales culture. Employees must receive frequent and concise information on their performance. The most effective feedback combines performance data and graphs, and simplifies the participant's performance in easily understood visuals—an invaluable medium in many high-performance banks. These banks depend on visuals to cut through complicated numerical trends and data, and to clearly illustrate performance versus targets. Graphs should be integrated into every sales report, wherever possible. Some banks enclose performance feedback reports with incentive checks, when payout occurs.

PLATFORM REPRESENTATIVE PERFORMANCE REPORT

NAME:	JOHN Q. PUBLIC			PERIOD MEASURED:	1/1/XX TO 1/31/XX
ID:	765432			DIVISION:	CENTRAL
LOCATION:	MAIN OFFICE			SUPERVISOR:	AAA

DESCRIPTION	GOAL	ACTUAL	WEIGHT	DESCRIPTION	GOAL	ACTUAL	WEIGHT
CUST. VOL./HR.	6.5	7.0	.10	TIME DEP. ROLL. %	84	87	.15
CROSS-SELL (NEW)	2.3	2.5	.15	NEW ACCOUNTS/HR.	11.5	12.3	.05
CROSS-SELL (EXIS.)	1.3	1.2	.15	PROM. PRODUCT VOL.	36	42	.05
FEE INCOME	1100	965	.05	KEY CUST. DEFECT. %	1.4	1.3	.10
QUAL. REFERRALS	15	21	.10	KEY CUST. SALES	12	14	.10

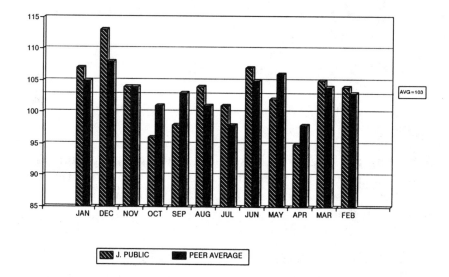

TOT. PERIOD PERFORMANCE	107.15%
TOT. PERIOD SALES POINTS	7.15
INCENTIVE PAY/POINTS	$ 30.00
SUBTOTAL	$ 214.50
PROMOT. PROD. BONUS	$ 23.00
INCENTIVE PAY EARNED	$ 237.50

CONGRATULATIONS ON YOUR EXCELLENT PERFORMANCE !!!!!
NEXT MONTH - EARN $5 EXTRA FOR EACH RETIREMENT
ACCOUNT OPENED. DON'T FORGET THE RAFFLE DRAWING
NEXT MONTH. FOR EVERY PERCENT ABOVE 100%, YOU WILL
RECEIVE AN ADDITIONAL ENTRY TICKET FOR THE DRAWING.
GOOD LUCK AND GOOD SELLING !!

Figure 7-1   Individual Performance Report

A sample performance feedback report is shown in Figure 7–1. The feedback report should contain, as a minimum, the performance of the individual against the bank average by:

- Total incentive points, both for the most recent period and the year to date, including total volume points, applicable overrides, and bonus points for any current promotional programs.
- Volume by total period, derived by multiplying the assigned weights of each product by the number of products sold.
- Volume by total product, with assigned weights next to each product according to its profitability.
- Cross-sell ratio, if applicable, with new customer and existing customer ratios calculated separately.
- Referral levels and quality, in percentages closed during the current period.
- Historical performance in at least the previous 6 measured periods. Historical performance, often the preferred item in the graph, typically illustrates the past 6 to 12 periods of overall performance, in bar graph form.

☐ EVALUATING INDIVIDUAL PERFORMANCE FEEDBACK

When an effective feedback system is in place, the bank can pinpoint specific areas in which performance can be improved. If an individual's percentage of cross-sell volume for a certain product is below average, the feedback report states this information and allows the bank to provide specific product knowledge training for that individual. Equally important, the feedback system indicates the individuals who have performed exceptionally well and should receive praise and rewards. It is important to fully train both the employees who receive the reports and their managers in the proper reading and interpretation of the results. Managers should receive individual employee reports and departmental or branch summary reports. These data can be used by managers in deciding on the focus of training, sales meetings, and promotions. The feedback report provides a powerful management tool; if used properly, it can increase performance and profitability.

❏ ESTABLISHING AN INFORMATION DISTRIBUTION SYSTEM

Vital to high-performance sales culture is an information distribution system. The system is typically administered by the Marketing Department or by the sales support manager (if one exists), who accumulates information and disseminates it in bulletins. Copies are sent to each employee and the employee's name is printed on every copy.

The bulletins are not meant to replace the bank's general newsletter but rather to serve as the primary information distribution tool, with the newsletter remaining a powerful supplement. Better than a newsletter, the bulletins provide in-depth information on specific topics by breaking up information into different issues at various times during the month instead of crowding all of it into one newsletter. They avoid the information delays of the newsletter, which is usually sent out only monthly or bi-weekly. The bulletins can be sent out within a day, if needed. Each subject bulletin is assigned a color code and is always printed on its designated color of paper. Assigning colors simplifies the building of useful files by the recipients. Table 7–1 highlights the most common information distribution system bulletin types.

❏ SALES ACHIEVEMENT BULLETIN

The sales achievement bulletin, which serves a unique purpose, should be separate from all other newsletters, bulletins, and house organs. This bulletin usually begins with a list of all personnel who are *above* their target quotas, as ranked by percentage over quota. Usually, both their percentages above quota and their locations appear next to their names. The list also distinguishes different departments and areas, providing one ranked list for the top platform representatives, one list for the top

Table 7–1   Information Distribution System

SALES ACHIEVEMENT BULLETIN: This bulletin highlights the year-to-date achievements of all sales representatives who have achieved above-average results. It is typically segregated by department or function (i.e., platform representatives, branch managers, commercial officers, trust officers, etc.). It then lists the achievers and states the percentage over year-to-date goals which each has achieved, beginning with the top performer and continuing on down to the better-than-average performer (even listing those at 101 percent). The bulletin briefly congratulates any employee who brought in any very noticeable business within the current month (i.e., a trust officer or commercial officer who landed a critical piece of business, etc.) and then provides highlights or sales tips from perhaps 2 or 3 of the top performers. Finally, it congratulates all for a job well done! This bulletin is sent out monthly.

COMPETITIVE INFORMATION BULLETIN: This bulletin focuses on all current offers and strategic programs at competing banks, thrifts, and other financial institutions which could possibly be a threat. It analyzes the product and the institution from which information originates, points out specific weaknesses of the product or campaign, and provides specific countermeasure techniques that can be used by the bank's contact people, to allow them to informatively discuss competitive products and be able to point out specific ways in which the bank's products, services, and "total offer" provide a better solution. This is done in all areas, especially Retail, Trust, and Commercial. These bulletins are issued as often as 2 to 3 times per month, when competitive information is received by any department or when originated from the Marketing Department.

CUSTOMER FEEDBACK BULLETIN: This bulletin focuses on customer feedback from all sources (i.e., defection analysis reports, customer surveys, etc.). It is imperative that all relevant managers and customer contact employees be aware of key service and product issues. This bulletin is also used to post daily, weekly, or monthly performance results of key service and product areas that the bank has identified as critical through customer feedback.

Table 7–1 (continued)

PRODUCT INFORMATION BULLETIN: This bulletin focuses on existing products, reviews strengths and weakness of the product, and provides details on the product which are commonly misunderstood yet important to the correct marketing of the product. Product information bulletins are an excellent way to increase product knowledge throughout the bank. The bulletin identifies the common characteristics of the target market so that the bank's contact people can recognize the need of such a product when in contact with prime candidates. Information should also be presented as to how to make a referral, including key contact names within the relevant department. Product information bulletins are often sent out 2 to 3 times per month.

PERSONNEL INFORMATION BULLETIN: This bulletin announces all promotions within the bank, especially highlighting key people within the organization who are given a change in functions. It often touches briefly on their background. Occasionally, Human Resources might post positions that have remained open, in spite of normal job posting and other sources, and will request any referrals or applications from in or outside of the bank.

MARKETING INFORMATION BULLETIN: This bulletin is different from the product information bulletins, in that it deals with new products and features or highlights a forthcoming promotion on certain products. In essence, it serves as an educational tool that orients the bank's personnel to the features and benefits of any new products or changes to existing products. When a marketing promotion is coming, it will highlight the products being promoted, show the advertisement or offer that was made, and provide recommended strategies to maximize any customer inquiries into the product or promotion. This bulletin is sent out on an as-needed frequency basis.

SPECIAL BULLETIN: This bulletin serves to address various needs within the bank, such as management announcement of new strategic moves or policies, or other topics. This bulletin is also sent out on an as-needed frequency basis.

---

branch managers, one for the top commercial officers, and so on. Anyone who is below 100 percent should not be on the list. It is meant to be a positive tool, citing all above-average achievers.

Citations and pictures, when possible, of employees who performed exceptionally well in the past several weeks should also be included. In addition, the bulletin should list bonus awards, prizes, and incentives for the next several months and should typically close with motivational remarks and a list of upcoming events and contests.

☐ COMPETITIVE INFORMATION BULLETIN

The marketing department of most high-performance banks provides a centralized point through which all competitive information funnels. The primary sources of competitive information are a bank's own relationship managers and customer contact employees. Three factors greatly impact continued employee contribution and the overall success of a centralized competitive information clearing house:

1. Each employee who contributes information must be recognized or cited as the source.
2. The information received must be distributed to the field rapidly.
3. The delivery mechanism must be simple to use and low in cost.

Using the competitive information bulletin, described in Table 7-1, the Marketing Department distributes information from a variety of sources. These may include:

Relationship managers and employees	Telephone inquiries to competitors
Customer defection analysis	Shopping of competitors
Direct customer feedback	Public relations announcements
Customer and noncustomer surveys	

Customer and noncustomer focus groups

Television commercials

Competitor employee interviews

Radio commercials

Newspaper advertisements

Direct mail

Periodical advertisements

Special-event publicity

❏ POSTING PERFORMANCE RESULTS

Charting and displaying individual sales performance in common employee areas is an effective tool for increasing performance. Most posted charts are large, they use graphics, and they are placed in common areas such as lunch rooms, main hallways, and other employee gathering areas. Such charts provide sales performance comparisons of all relevant employees, by name. Charts are also frequently used in sales competitions, as a source of continuous feedback to all employees.

❏ CUSTOMER FEEDBACK

In improving the performance of a sales culture, one of the first steps is to pinpoint problem areas as they are perceived by customers. All customer contact employees should be trained in how to collect customer information and feedback, what actions to take, and where the information is to be sent. Distribution of customer feedback information should be formalized in a customer feedback bulletin. Several banks pay their customers cash on the spot for turning in a suggestion letter or form.

Studies and surveys should be used to identify and prioritize service and product areas that need to be improved. Customer feedback should be used to identify those services that customers find most critical. Ranking and prioritizing product and service deficiencies allows senior management to maximize the impact of the resources the bank has reinvested in improving service. This information should be integrated into employees' goals, performance standards, and incentive plans. The most common customer feedback tools are:

Closed account surveys

New account surveys

Defection analysis reports

Service quality surveys

Customer satisfaction surveys

Suggestion boxes

Wholesale relationship surveys

Customer/noncustomer focus groups

Shopper programs (not true customer feedback)

Customer comment cards

Customer complaint numbers

❏ BREAKING DOWN FEEDBACK BARRIERS

Getting accurate customer feedback is challenging, but it is essential to building a sales culture. Numerous studies have shown that only a fraction of customers complain when they are dissatisfied with a service. Breaking down communication barriers to increase customer feedback is vital to keeping these customers. The following suggestions should be integrated into an overall service quality program:

- Provide direct and easy methods to register complaints. Many customers fail to complain because they do not know whom to contact. The bank should periodically mail letters pledging quality service. Appropriate contacts to call, if service ever falls below expectations, should be included in these letters. Pledges naming these contacts should be a part of the account opening process. Departmental customer service *and* complaint hotline numbers should be provided in every statement.

- Create an atmosphere in which customers feel that the bank is responsive and takes action on customer feedback. On the retail side, some banks pay cash on the spot for any new suggestions. All traceable complaints receive written responses detailing the action taken or the reason why action was not appropriate.

- Train all customer contact employees who handle complaints, to ensure a nonconfrontational experience for the customer. The customer should *always* be thanked for the complaint because it has given the bank an opportunity to improve its operations. Anonymous complaint paths should also be available to customers who are apprehensive about possible retaliation or estrangement from affected bank employees.

❑ WHOLESALE RELATIONSHIP SURVEYS

Surveys of commercial banking customers and other wholesale banking clients reveal interesting and often surprising results. When wholesale customers are questioned about how often they would like to be called on, respondents indicate a preference for a much higher contact rate than relationship managers normally expect. These surveys indicate that most companies are highly receptive to increased attention by their banks. Unfortunately, banks are commonly increasing the workload of their relationship managers. Because of the greater numbers of customers assigned to each relationship manager, meeting a customer's preferred contact rate is often difficult.

Several banks require their officers to make a certain number of normal customer calls and rapid contacts per week. Rapid contacts involve meeting with or calling customers for a brief period (under 10 minutes) to say hello, build a stronger relationship, and continuously monitor the customer's condition. This intermittent contact between actual calls is highly effective in cementing loyalty. The customer eventually views the relationship manager as a friend and business partner, not just a calling officer on a yearly review. Guess which bank will become or remain the company's lead bank, all other factors being equal?

❏ IMPROVING SHOPPER FEEDBACK

Shopper programs have been widely instituted, with great success. It is extremely important that the shopper service be used to its full potential because of the cost "per shop" and the feedback. To motivate employees, a number of banks award cash bonuses to those employees who perform well while being shopped. An employee should receive the shopper feedback, usually in written form, when that employee receives the check or cash incentive. Ideally, the check or cash should be presented at the weekly or monthly departmental or branch sales meeting, after the manager discusses the positive comments on the feedback form. Negative comments on the evaluation sheet should be left for the employee to read privately; the evaluator should always list one area for improvement. Shopper feedback, which is intended to measure performance against stated criteria, should not be confused with customer feedback. Trained researchers with their own biases and objectives are providing feedback, not the customers. This was the approach used by one bank:

> When an individual shopping evaluation is below average, our branch managers do not single out the employee at the next sales meeting. Rather, our managers are instructed to use the poor performance rating as an opportunity to improve service throughout the branch. The managers accomplish this by explaining that, because a shopper has given one of the employees an unsatisfactory rating in a certain area, specific training will help all employees to consistently rate high as a group. Role play and practice sessions follow the instruction, to ensure retention. In this way, the low performer is not singled out or embarrassed in a group situation, and everyone learns from the feedback. Discreet review of the evaluation form and individual coaching of the particular employee take place after the group training, in a supportive and positive manner.

Shoppers should also notice patterns among the employees they evaluate. Regular reports should be submitted to the training department, managers, and marketing area, detailing those topics and areas in which the bank's employees experience the most difficulty. Shoppers must also be trained to spot and report operational problems that impact service or performance, such as time-consuming paperwork and unnecessary procedures.

❑ INTERDEPARTMENTAL REFERRAL FORMS

In measuring performance standards, interdepartmental referrals should be a requirement for all bank employees who are in contact with customers. Branch managers, commercial officers, trust officers, and other high-contact employees are consistently presented with opportunities to make referrals to each other and to other departments. Unfortunately, many banks do not formally train their employees to identify opportunities and make useful referrals. To compound the problem, standard interdepartmental referral systems often do not exist, resulting in lost opportunities. If the departments are not automated, simple forms should be created for the exchange and tracking of referrals. A sample form is shown in Figure 7–2(a) and 7–2(b).

Referral frequency goals should be jointly set with employees and measured as part of their performance appraisals. In addition, their sales and product knowledge training should include training on interdepartmental referrals. Well-developed referral systems directly increase teamwork, revenue, and profitability.

❑ IMPROVING BANK TELEPHONE DIRECTORIES

One of the most essential skills a new employee learns is where to seek information and who can answer questions and get things done in various departments. Employees should have direct contacts in all developments, to make referrals and to receive timely and accurate information on products, services and policies. Several banks have expanded their bank directories to include primary and secondary liaison contacts in each department. These designated liaisons answer product or service questions and relay referrals. Some banks provide each employee with liaison-name binders that are updated regularly and sorted by topic area for easy reference.

Referral

Customer Name: _____   To: _____

Phone: _____   Dept: _____

Street: _____   Location: _____

City, State, Zip: _____   From: _____

Company Name (if applicable): _____   Employee ID: _____

Title (if applicable): _____   Location: _____

Products interested in: _____   Phone: _____

_____   Date: _____

_____   Special Instructions: _____

- -

(to be completed by bank employee following up)

Employee Name: _____   Products sold: _____

Employee ID: _____   Products pending: _____

Date received: _____   Follow-up date: _____

Spoke to: _____   Action step: _____

Products interested in: _____   Signature: _____

Figure 7–2(a)   Interdepartmental Referral Form

```
┌─────────────────────────────────────────────────────────────────┐
│                          Referral                                 │
│                                                                   │
│  I would like to introduce:                                       │
│                              _____ │
│                                                                   │
│  who would like information on:                                   │
│                              _____ │
│                                                                   │
│                              _____ │
│                                                                   │
│  By: _____  Employee ID: _____  Branch: ____│
│                                                                   │
│  Opened Account Type: _____  Account #: _____  Opening $: _│
│                                                                   │
│  Opened Account Type: _____  Accont #: _____  Opening $: _│
└─────────────────────────────────────────────────────────────────┘
```

Figure 7–2(b)   Teller Referral Form

8

Noncash Incentives

If a bank truly wants to motivate employees to increase performance, then logic dictates that the bank should link selling behavior with positive rewards. Those rewards can be in such different forms as monetary incentives, distinction and recognition, additional vacation and benefits, or increased personal satisfaction. The important concept here is that positive selling behavior *must* lead to a direct and timely response, from the bank, that makes a significant and positive impact.

❏ PERSONAL MOTIVATOR SURVEY

How can an individual best be motivated, if a manager does not know which of the possible rewards offered—cash incentives, recognition, praise, time off, trips, prizes—an employee values most? Predictably, cash incentives will be awarded to an employee who would much rather receive travel and recognition, or vice versa. A costly mistake? Yes.

Several banks have addressed this problem by administering a *personal motivator survey*. The individual ranks the most attractive types of rewards and their degree of magnitude. These surveys may be supplemented by personal interviews, meetings, and on-the-job observance so that managers can gain the basic information they need to properly motivate and reward each employee. A reward-and-motivation system can then be constructed and tailored to each individual, ensuring the maximum impact. It can be a costly mistake to assume that all employees are motivated equally by cash incentives or other specific rewards. A sample survey is reproduced in Figure 8–1.

❏ FORMALIZING SENIOR MANAGEMENT RECOGNITION

Although most managers realize that recognition is a strong motivator, few banks have established a routine recognition program for sales excellence. Several high-performance banks have senior managers who regularly review sales results at all levels and send out daily "job-well-done" memos to line employees who perform well. This senior management recognition system sends a clear signal to all employees that sales performance results are carefully reviewed and rewarded.

Banks whose presidents or CEOs praise sales performers on a regular basis find that recognition is highly motivating and confirms senior management's commitment to a sales culture. To ensure that employees are recognized regularly, the president or CEO is provided with a list of top performers every week (usually 2 to 10 individuals, depending on the size of the bank). Recognition is given in a personal visit to the employee's office, or by telephone or in a letter. The employee's co-workers should be present, to ensure that the recognition is effective and to make a visible statement of support for the sales culture.

❏ EFFECTIVE INTERNAL PROMOTIONALS

There are countless ways to recognize top performers. Successful internal promotionals are tailored to individual rewards through motivational surveys, as discussed above. Table 8–1 highlights several common rewards for superior sales performance.

A quick budgeting rule-of-thumb is to allocate internal promotionals for 10 to 15 percent of all funds appropriated for sales

Name: _____ Date: _____

Title: _____ Supervisor: _____

Dept./Location: _____ Employee ID: _____

Please rank questions 1 through 9 in alphabetical order from the most important (A) to the least important (I):

1. _____ A professional career
2. _____ Income potential
3. _____ Opportunity to advance into management
4. _____ Earnings are related to performance
5. _____ Flexibility in work schedule
6. _____ Working with people
7. _____ This type of work matches my skills
8. _____ Helping people by providing a service
9. _____ Job security
10. _____ Other factor: _____

Please rank questions 11 through 21 from most preferred (A) to least preferred (K) methods of being rewarded for exceptional performance (assume all rewards are of equal monetary value where applicable):

11. _____ Events, dinners, game or show tickets
12. _____ Cash
13. _____ Gifts, merchandise, catalog certificates
14. _____ Travel prizes and airline tickets
15. _____ Plaques, awards, certificates
16. _____ Recognition in front of peers
17. _____ Recognition in front of senior managers
18. _____ "Thank You" by direct supervisor
19. _____ Admittance to "Top Performers" club
20. _____ Days off
21. _____ No reward wanted
22. At this point, how much increase over your current personal earnings would satisfy you?
    a. Don't need an increase
    b. Less than 10%
    c. 10 to 20%
    d. 21 to 30%
    e. 31 to 50%
    f. 51 to 75%
    g. 76 to 100%
    h. Over 100%

Figure 8–1   Personal Goals and Motivators Survey

23. How many hours of work per week do you feel is appropriate for your position?
    a. Under 25 hours
    b. 25–35 hours
    c. 36 to 40 hours
    d. 41 to 45 hours
    e. 46 to 50 hours
    f. 51 to 55 hours
    g. 56 to 60 hours
    h. Over 60 hours
24. How important is it for you to have the opportunity to go into management?
    a. Very important
    b. Somewhat important
    c. Of average importance
    d. Of little importance
    e. Not important at all
25. How adequate is the income you receive from your current job?
    a. Not adequate for minimum living essentials
    b. Just adequate for minimum essentials
    c. Adequate for decent living standard
    d. More than adequate to live comfortably
26. How would you rate your chances for advancement or improvement in you present job?
    a. Very good
    b. Good
    c. Fair
    d. Poor
    e. Very poor
27. Which of the following best describes the security that is offered by your current job?
    a. Very secure
    b. Somewhat secure
    c. About average security
    d. Somewhat insecure
    e. Very insecure
28. List your two top short-term business goals:
    _____
    _____
29. List your two top long-term business goals:
    _____
    _____
30. Name the position in which you hope to be employed in:
    2 Years: _____
    5 Years: _____
31. List your two top personal goals:
    _____
    _____

Figure 8–1 (*continued*)

Table 8-1 Common Internal Sales Promotionals

Dinner cooked by president or CEO An entertaining evening for the employee and a fun method for senior management to show commitment to the sales effort.

Boat rides For those near water, a boat ride often includes dinner, and the spouse is usually invited. Senior management is present and an awards ceremony is usually held.

Luxury car for a month The bank leases an expensive luxury car and each month allows a top sales performer to use the car.

Sweepstakes Entry tickets are earned based on sales. Weekly winners are drawn for small prizes. A "Super Sweepstakes Winner" is awarded the grand prize at the end.

Limousine service The bank provides the top weekly or monthly sales performer with limousine service to and from work each day, during the following week or month.

Auctions Fake money is awarded, based on sales performance. At the end of each period, an auction is held with real prizes— the highest bidders win the merchandise and pay with the fake money.

President's parking spot Top performers are allowed to park in the president's parking spot for a month (or the applicable manager's space, if not a main-office location).

Recognition breakfasts Monthly breakfasts with the CEO, for top performers.

Event tickets A less expensive method of promotion, often featuring movie passes, show performances, or sporting events, when appropriate.

Flowers for a month Flowers delivered to the employee's desk every day for a month.

Table 8-1 (*continued*)

Shopping spree Bank credit card with a preassigned limit, issued to winning employees who "shop to their limits."

Merchandise Items such as watches and crystal are popular. Watches and rings often have spaces for several diamonds, awarded individually for excellent performance.

ATM withdrawal Bank employees are given an ATM card and allowed to withdraw as much money as possible over 5 minutes (one at a time).

Traditional awards Trophies, pins, pens, and plaques are still excellent methods of recognition.

Airline tickets Tickets can be effective motivational awards and are usually for tropical destinations such as the Caribbean or the Hawaiian Islands.

Dinners for two Gift certificates for the finest restaurants in town.

Catalog certificates This campaign is especially effective when a broad coverage of employees is wanted. It is often based on points earned in special sales promotions.

incentives and rewards. Internal promotional prizes should be targeted at the very top 1 to 2 percent of all performers, allowing the bank to offer substantial rewards to these employees.

☐ MOTIVATING MEMOS

Often, the least expensive alternative can achieve the highest motivational effect. Motivating memos are an excellent medium for recognizing individual performance. To maximize the effectiveness of these memos, several guidelines exist. Vague or lengthy memos praising general excellent performance should be avoided. Ideally, the memos should be very specific and should consist of no more than two paragraphs. The first paragraph should briefly summarize the specific performance. The second paragraph should explain how the bank benefited from it and should contain a sentence or two of praise for the employee. A courtesy copy of the memo should be sent to the employee's direct manager or supervisor, the sales support manager, and the Human Resources Department, for inclusion in the employee's files.

❑ SALES PERFORMER CLUBS

A number of high-performance banks have heralded elite *sales performer clubs* for playing a crucial and visible role in enhancing their sales cultures. Of all bank employees with sales responsibility, typically 10 percent earn the right to be considered club members. The club is usually given a name, such as "Master's Circle" or a similarly enticing title. Membership in this club qualifies the employees for special rewards, recognition, and a year-end holiday banquet. When an employee is inducted into the club, a ceremony is conducted by the CEO, at the club banquet. The banquet is often held at a neighboring resort, where the member-employees and their spouses are hosted for 2 to 3 days, with all expenses covered. Club membership is marked by desk plaques, pins, and the imprint of the club's symbol on the member's business cards. A committee is frequently elected by the club to discuss ways of increasing bankwide sales effectiveness and to make recommendations to senior management which, if implemented, would turn this group into a *sales advisory committee*. Sales performer club membership is an excellent reward for sales performance. Here are a leading bank's comments:

> In addition to our sales recognition club, we established a top tier within the club for the highest 1 to 2 percent of all sales performers. Induction into this club entitles the candidate to a meal with the chairman of the board as well as other monetary and gift incentives above the normal club status. At the end of the year, we host the chairman's meal at a luxurious resort to which those who

qualify for the top-tier club receive an all-expenses-paid one-week stay with transportation. The top-tier club allows us to spend lavishly on our very best performers, yet to contain internal sales promotional costs to a reasonable amount. In fact, the increased profitability of our star performers alone covers the club's expense. Lifetime membership status can be achieved by making either club five times.

❏ EMPLOYEE PERQUISITES

Senior management perquisites are frequently awarded temporarily to line employees as a reward for sales excellence. Given to high performers for periods ranging from 1 week to 1 year, perquisites provide an excellent tool to motivate and distinguish performance. Table 8–2 lists perquisites used as rewards for achievement or as prizes for internal promotional programs.

❏ SALES MANAGER REWARD FUND

An inherent problem in bonus and incentive systems is the long delay, often weeks or months, between behavior and reward. Several banks have addressed this problem by augmenting their incentive plans with a *sales manager reward fund*. Here is an example:

> Each of our line managers is given a designated amount of money per employee to use for motivational rewards each year. The managers can use the money at their complete discretion, to reward their employees. We provide basic guidelines, such as giving out at least one award per month. A list of effective and proven ideas to motivate employees with the fund is distributed to our managers. The reward fund has been extremely successful in immediately rewarding excellence. Our managers are able to provide personalized awards and prizes during the weekly or monthly sales meetings.

❏ SPOUSES AS MOTIVATORS

A valuable aid in motivating married employees is the influence of their spouses. When possible, rewards should include

Table 8–2 Common Perquisites Used as Sales Achievement Rewards

---

Memberships

Health club
Luncheon club
Country club
Buyers' club
Dinner and speaker clubs
Association dues

Facilities and Equipment Privileges

Reserved parking
Executive dining room
Company car
Limousine service

Services, Seminars, and Counseling

Financial counseling and seminars
Flexible personal loans
Waiver of mortgage points and fees
Income tax preparation
Annual financial planning
Legal counseling
Physical exams/Counseling
Sabbatical leaves

Travel and Entertainment

Reserved box at theaters
Tickets to sporting events
Tickets to movies
First-class tickets
Airline club privileges
Spouse airline tickets

---

participation by the spouse. When dinners or other award events are held, the spouse should be included. When contests or other internal promotionals are scheduled, internal marketing material should be sent to all employees' homes, to increase awareness and encouragement by spouses.

❑ SPECIAL TELLER PROMOTIONALS

The number of internal promotional programs that can be implemented is infinite. Here are two interesting programs:

1. Coins-in-the-Jar. Tellers are given a set amount of money in coins each month. The coins are kept in a glass jar or an attractive container, between the teller and the customer. Each jar contains the teller's name. Should the teller not smile, call the customer by name, serve the customer courteously, or mention the availability of a featured product, the customer can take a coin from the container. The teller with the most coins at the end of the month is recognized, and all tellers are allowed to keep the coins remaining at the end of each month.

2. Referral Slip Bonus. When teller referral volume is not meeting target goals, a 1-month teller referral bonus can often assist. Rewards can include additional cash incentives, gifts, or even a raffle drawing in which each referral slip earns tickets for the grand drawing. Total referral goals for tellers should also be evaluated as part of branch manager performance appraisals.

9

Incentive Pay for Performance

The main purpose of an incentive plan is to increase long-term bank profitability, not to increase employee pay. The beauty of a properly designed incentive plan is that it does both. The primary objective of incentive plans is to increase margins and revenues over the cost of incentives. The following ideas have enhanced the effectiveness of properly designed incentive plans.

❏ ADMINISTERING CAFETERIA INCENTIVES

Numerous types of *incentive compensation plans* (ICPs) exist. Most banks originally offered salary-plus-commission plans. Then, after adding thresholds, they progressed to *gain-sharing plans* at the line level and *profit-sharing* plans at the executive level. Banks with highly developed internal cost accounting systems administer hybrid gain-sharing plans based on profitability at the individual level.

Cafeteria plans are gaining in popularity. These combine several different short-term incentives (STIs) and/or long-term incentives (LTIs) which, together, achieve the desired motivational effect. Cafeteria plans are commonly used for commercial loan offices, where it is desirable to use an individual gain-sharing plan for fee-based income generation, a team gain-sharing or profit-sharing plan to ensure loan quality, and long-term incentives to encourage retention.

The design of each cafeteria plan mix should be based on a personal motivators survey (discussed earlier) and on the particular incentive needs of each position. In some of these plans, employees are allowed to choose, within limits, the types of incentives they can aim for. However, simplicity is a key to the success of any incentive compensation plan. Table 9–1 highlights some common incentives.

❏ CORPORATE REFERRAL COMMISSION PLAN

The ability to capitalize on referrals is essential to profitability. A number of high-performance banks have instituted corporationwide referral commission plans in which every employee is eligible, regardless of position, department, or division. In these programs, a flat fee or commission rate is calculated for each product and department. A handbook is then created, listing every bank service or product by description, features, benefits, typical prospects, the individual who must approve referrals, and the commission amount or range. These referral handbooks are comprehensive and can include products from the bank's brokerage, real estate, asset-based lending, insurance, and other subsidiaries. The handbook is distributed to every employee.

Product knowledge training based on this handbook is selective; individual managers can focus on the products most appropriate for the customers they serve. Employees in areas deemed capable of providing the highest level of referrals are given formalized training based on the handbook; managers of all other employees are simply expected to review the handbook with them. Commissions are paid centrally on all legitimate referrals that result in closed business. Videotapes and other means of internal marketing are also frequently utilized.

❏ BANK PAY STRATEGIES

Several surveys have shown that average banks compensate their employees at a *higher* level of base pay than top-performing

Table 9-1   Incentive Compensation Plans (ICPs)

Plan	Description
Cafeteria Plan	A tailored and balanced ICP that incorporates a variety of different incentives for maximum effectiveness.
Short-Term Incentives (STIs)	ICP with complete payout of 1 year or under, without stock.

Commission
  Straight commission
  Draw against commission
  Salary plus commission
	Simple payout based on sales volume. Frequently a first step in offering an ICP, a salary-plus-commission plan is usually adopted for recruiting and stability reasons. By improving their original commission plans with thresholds and other features, many banks have in actuality progressed to gain-sharing and profit-sharing plans (see below).

Gain Sharing
  Individual
  Team
	Payout when an individual, a department, or a unit surpasses a predetermined performance target. This is one of the most common and effective bank ICPs. Gain-sharing plans are the most popular ICPs in banks today. Many include both individual and team gain sharing, to maximize both individual accountability and teamwork.

Lump-Sum Bonus Discretionary	One-time cash payment based on individual or group

Table 9-1 (*continued*)

Plan	Description
Fixed formula basis Peer group performance basis Plan basis Qualitative performance basis Quantitative performance basis	performance. The bonus does not necessarily need to be repeated, nor does it become part of base pay.
Pay-for-Knowledge	An increase in base salary, dependent on the number of duties or tasks an individual can perform within the bank. This plan is not linked to performance in the present position.
Profit Sharing Salary based Qualitative performance based Quantitative performance based	ICP based directly on corporate profits, typically on an annual or quarterly basis. To be effective, the eligible employees must be able to make an impact on the bank's profit. Profit-sharing plans will increase in popularity as bank sophistication and cost accounting improve at the department/area/individual level.
Long-Term Incentives (LTIs) Incentive stock options plans (ISOP) Performance share/unit plan Phantom stock plan Nonqualified stock option plan Restricted stock plan Stock appreciation rights plan	LTI strategies usually include basing rewards on stock ownership or options. The intent is to focus the employee on long-term well-being and gain of the corporation. LTIs take many forms, some of which are listed here.

banks do. This policy cripples profitability during market changes, by locking in a high level of fixed payroll overhead. On average, top-performing banks compensate their employees 4 to 10 percent less in base salaries, with incentives tied heavily to profitability. These high performers pay out a higher-than-average total compensation (base plus incentives) during favorable market conditions. They have increased flexibility and adaptability during market changes, because their fixed overhead is significantly lower than that of their competitors. During drops in bank profitability, the compensation of the lowest performers is most affected. Increased attrition of low performers, especially in soft markets, lessens the need for layoffs and other cost-cutting measures.

❏ CREATING GOLDEN HANDCUFFS

One key objective of incentive pay systems is to retain top producers. A tool used by a few banks is the creation of golden handcuffs at the line level. By retaining 20 to 50 percent of each employee's eligible incentives and paying these out over a period of several years, a bank can offer its top producers a continual yearly escalation in incentive pay. More importantly, top producers might forfeit so much incentive pay, if they were to leave, that most decide to remain for the long term.

❏ GUIDELINES FOR A SUCCESSFUL PLAN

Several general guidelines apply to designing and implementing a successful incentive pay plan. These are listed in Table 9–2.

❏ MANAGER CONDITIONAL PAYOUT INCENTIVES

One downfall of incentive pay lies with management compensation. If a branch or department has several top producers, overall profitability or other goals may be met or surpassed despite the many low performers. If a manager can count on these top producers, there is less incentive to work with and improve the low performers. By requiring that a certain *percentage* of the

Table 9–2   Incentive Plan Guidelines

- Design simplicity is vital. The targeted employees must be able to easily understand the program. Design simplicity also makes the program easy to administer and track.

- The system should be automated, relying on existing databases and account numbers to minimize administrative tasks and provide a readily audited system. Improperly structured incentive pay plans cannot be easily managed and administrated. Nonautomation of many sections often results in a program fraught with administrative problems. Such systems also suffer from reporting inaccuracies, and simple yet effective auditing procedures are needed to identify nonreporting and inaccuracies.

- The incentive system should be adaptable: the same system should be able to accommodate the tracking and payout of incentives for many different and concurrent incentive plans, promotionals, bonuses, and part-time employees. Most successful systems rely on points. Payout is based on total accumulated points, divided by days or hours worked.

- The incentive plan should compensate for a wide range of sales and service quality goals. If incentive plans are too limited in scope, activities not compensated for will suffer. Many banks integrate service quality and other goals into incentive systems.

- Individual product profitability should be the basis for incentive points or credit awarded to employees for selling a product. This will encourage employees to promote and sell products that are most profitable for the bank. When the contribution margin of each product is not known or traceable, some banks have used expert opinions by senior managers.

- Threshold criteria should be established for payout. Incentive plans without thresholds are often viewed as too expensive to keep in place.

Table 9–2 (*continued*)

- Incentives should be based on factors that the individual being measured can control to a great degree, and should be offered to *all* individuals who can control or influence results (i.e., on the retail side, *both* branch managers and platform representatives should be motivated to achieve total deposit growth).

- The incentives chosen should be sufficient to motivate employees. Although basic, this guideline is commonly violated. Goals are set to unrealistic levels for average performers, resulting in demotivation of what should be the primary targets of the incentive plan.

- Visible management support and an effective educational campaign to ensure understanding of the incentives are crucial. Lack of either will signal to employees that the program will likely be temporary or is of little consequence.

department's or branch's sales representatives meet or exceed specific standards before an incentive is paid to the manager, a bank can ensure that the manager will take an active role in improving all employees.

❏ INCENTIVE OVERRIDES FOR MANAGERS

A number of banks report great success in providing *incentive overrides* to line managers, based on line sales representative performance. The overrides are commonly a percentage of total sales incentives paid to the managers' direct employees. Because a portion of each line manager's income depends on the line sales team, each line manager takes a direct and visible interest in ensuring peak performance from each member of the team.

❏ TRAINEE INCENTIVES

Measuring both trainees and experienced employees by the same performance criteria virtually ensures that all employees will be discouraged by the bank's incentive system in their first few quarters of employment. This outcome inevitably affects each employee's opinion of a sales position as a career. It is important to have a trainee incentive system that rewards new employees based on their efforts. Only after a reasonable period should they be measured on results. Criteria that measure effort can include improvement in product knowledge, number of referrals or calls made, or other volume measures not overly dependent on experience.

❏ INTERDEPARTMENTAL TEAMWORK INCENTIVES

Territorial disputes between departments often obstruct the maximizing of total customer relationship profitability. A lack of both referral generation and referral follow-through further erodes bank margins. Several banks have based a portion of department manager incentives on total relationship profitability, to both increase total margins by customer and communicate the importance of cooperation and referrals to each line manager. *Interdepartmental teamwork incentives* compel managers to view the "big picture" of total bank profitability and to reinforce this concept through incentives and recognition.

❏ TELLER REFERRAL INCENTIVES

A problem often encountered by banks contemplating a referral program is a fear that there will be referral-count dishonesty, and that the bank will be forced to pay out on dishonest referrals or else to drop the program. On the retail side, an effective solution is to pay tellers 25 to 40 percent of any bonuses or incentives normally paid to a platform representative, when an account is opened as a result of the teller's referral. The advantage of splitting the money between the platform representative and teller is that the split ensures that referral levels will not be exaggerated, detracting from the platform representative's compensation. In addition, such a plan ensures a constant payout by the bank because it only pays out a certain fee for an opened account, regardless of whether a teller made the referral. The platform representatives also gain because they would not have otherwise opened the account. This system is especially simple when the bank uses product bundling and pays out a standard bonus on the successful sale of a package.

❏ RETIREMENT INCENTIVES

Targeted at middle- and upper-level officers, *retirement incentives* are an effective alternative to cash incentives. Usually earned on a point system, these incentives are geared toward adding to the retirement benefits each officer has already earned. Retirement incentives are effective in increasing officer retention and are often preferred over cash by executives looking to defer present income until retirement, for tax purposes.

❏ ESCALATING CROSS-SELL INCENTIVES

To encourage multiple product sales to the same customer, many banks offer *escalating cross-sell incentives*. For each additional product sold during a customer meeting, the relationship manager or platform representative receives a cash bonus. A relatively small cash incentive is paid out for the second product sold, a larger one for the third product sold and so on. Escalating cross-sell incentives typically supplement existing incentive-based programs which are often reduced and weighted for profitability.

❏ EXISTING CUSTOMER INCENTIVE BONUSES

Because a bank's primary and most cost-effective opportunity to generate additional business lies within its existing customer base, a number of top-performing banks have instituted special *existing customer incentive bonuses* on both the retail and wholesale sides. When a bank product or service is sold to an existing customer, the relationship manager is paid an additional bonus amount above the normal incentive, based on the product's average profitability.

❑ TELEMARKETING INCENTIVE BONUSES

To encourage proactive telemarketing efforts on the retail side, especially to upscale customers, several banks offer bonuses over and above normal incentives if a product or service is sold over the phone rather than in a branch visit.

❑ LOAN OFFICER INCENTIVES

Because of the inherent danger and conflict of interest in rewarding relationship managers based on loan volume, many banks have come up with alternatives to direct volume incentives. Several alternative strategies are described in Table 9–3.

Table 9–3 Loan Officer Incentive Strategies

> **GOAL: Inspire new business from targeted noncustomers.**
>
> *Strategy:* Provide bonuses based on the conversion of targeted accounts to customers, with incremental rewards dependent on volume, number of services used, or relationship profitability.
>
> **GOAL: Ensure that the loan officers are team players.**
>
> *Strategy:* Fund total incentive funds available based on the entire group's performance, and weight group performance heavily in calculating individual incentives. Provide additional bonuses based on business gained by joint calling.

Table 9–3 (*continued*)

GOAL: Increase level of coverage and frequency of calls to existing customers.

Strategy: Provide bonuses based on additional products, services, or volume levels sold to existing customers. Provide incentives for key account retention, and weight customer retention heavily in performance appraisals.

GOAL: Assure high quality of new loans.

Strategy: Pay incentives for new loans on a graduated scale, dependent on quality as determined by the credit area. Some banks also pay full incentives on strong loans and partial payout on marginal loans (full payout is delayed and adjusted for profitability).

GOAL: Increase referrals to other areas (i.e., trust, private banking, etc.).

Strategy: Provide bonuses based on qualified referrals to other departments. Establish monthly referral targets for each relationship manager, and weight performance heavily on performance appraisals.

GOAL: Assure proper follow-up on problem loans.

Strategy: Base incentives heavily on charge-offs and loan classifications. Provide incentives based on total portfolio profitability. Bonuses are also frequently paid for increasing the average portfolio quality, as measured by the loan review area.

GOAL: Increase retention of top-producing officers.

Strategy: Retain 20 to 50 percent of eligible incentives per employee and then disburse the retained funds over a period of several years. This has the effect of creating a golden handcuff annuity which officers forfeit if they leave premature.

❏ NONCONTACT STAFF INCENTIVES

Two major factors that determine the sales ability of relationship managers are the level and the quality of internal support. Administrators, support staff, marketing staff, information systems managers, and others often have a significant impact on the results relationship managers can achieve. Several progressive banks, in studies of their own noncontact staff operations, have identified positions that affect sales performance, and have established incentives based on functions that improve sales effectiveness. The incentives are based on satisfying the noncontact staff's clients—in this case, the relationship managers. Quality service, both internal and external, is crucial to bank profitability and must be quantified, measured, and rewarded.

Timely response to customer inquiries and problems is also essential to both sales and service functions. Several banks have addressed this issue by awarding incentive points based on the timeliness of individual or departmental responses. Time incentives are bolstered by quality incentives, to ensure both internal and external customer satisfaction. These incentives help ensure fulfillment of both prospective and existing customer service needs.

❏ ESCALATING INCENTIVES

To ensure that top retail and wholesale producers are always performing at their best levels, several banks have introduced escalating incentives. These additional incentives are based on cumulative volume over established thresholds. Three to four thresholds are typically established, and top producers earn a higher percentage amount over standard incentives each time they clear a new threshold. Volume totals are usually reset at the end of each fiscal year or other appropriate period.

❏ OUTSIDER INCENTIVES

Several banks, seeking to maximize referrals, have paid incentives to individuals outside of the bank. Outside referrals that lead to commercial loans or fee-based income, such as trust closings, asset management, cash management and private placements, are rewarded with pre-established commissions. This strategy is especially effective when banks are trying to break into a new market with limited contacts or networking opportunities. The payout scale is often graduated, based on profitability, volume, or amount. To encourage referrals that lead to lasting and profitable customer relationships, referral bonuses are paid out for each additional year the customer remains with the bank. (Amounts paid in subsequent years are substantially less than the initial payout amount.) Some banks augment traditional outsider incentives with immediate cash incentives for any qualified leads willing to meet with the bank's relationship manager to discuss specific products.

❏ THE IMPORTANCE OF A THRESHOLD

One of the largest barriers to an effective incentive pay plan is the fear by management that such a program will "lock-in" the bank to pay out more money than necessary to bring in business. Although most top executives are willing to risk some money during better fiscal years, on the chance that it will bring in further business in the long term, they hesitate to install a system that will trap them during bad years.

An incentive pay plan should only pay out when performance is over a "threshold" level. Although many incentive pay plans pay out partially before this threshold level, such plans face grave dangers during bad times, when top executives look for areas to cut spending. Because the result could severely undermine the sales culture evolution of the bank, a threshold incentive pay system works best in the long term. In addition, a threshold system has the advantage of not paying employees twice for the same level of work, (they would continue to bring in existing levels, without added incentives). The system also allows the bank to pay relatively larger incentives on the additional volume that would not have been possible if it were paying for existing volume as well. In brief, senior management has nothing to lose and a great deal to gain by launching a threshold incentive pay system in which profits not seen otherwise are split with employees.

❏ SETTING A THRESHOLD LEVEL

The most accurate and common method of determining threshold levels is the use of historical data. On either the corporate or retail side, historical data are usually readily available. Three distinct methods to set thresholds are: standardized bankwide performance criteria based on position averages, personalized goals based on individual past performance, and individual goals broken down and distributed from senior management targets. Adjustments should be made from the chosen foundation, depending on local market conditions and other known environmental factors that impact volume and profitability within a defined geographic region.

Other factors to consider include the number of new employees in a branch or department and the level of staffing in comparison to previous years. Many banks exclude the performance of new employees from the measurements, so that they will not unfavorably impact the incentive compensation of the department or branch. Typical exclusion periods range from 45 to 90 days on the retail side, and from to 180 to 360 days on the wholesale side. If implementation of new systems or equipment will impact employee productivity, then adjustments to the foundation will again need to be made.

It is essential that the threshold level not be so overly aggressive as to discourage employees from ever reaching it. On the other hand, it must not be too easily achieved, or the bank will be paying the employees twice for a level of performance that they would have achieved without the incentives. The threshold level must be an unbiased estimate of what could be expected if performance levels remained the same, which forces employees to improve performance in order to earn incentives.

❏ APPROACHING EMPLOYEES WITH INCENTIVES

A delicate issue for employees who are not used to being paid incentives or commissions is the method by which the plan is implemented. Although some banks have cut base salaries and shown employees how to "make up the difference" with incentives, this approach arouses skepticism and fear among employees.

Most banks progress from a conservative system of allocating a capped total dollar amount for incentives to a more aggressive plan, once the employees have become adjusted to the incentive system. Such banks have then smoothly implemented an aggressive gain-sharing or incentive plan by freezing base salaries and introducing incentives to compensate for any differences thereby avoiding threatening salary reductions.

Education is a key to smoothly implementing an incentive plan. Several banks have their senior officers conduct bandwagon "tours," meeting with groups of the affected employees to explain how the system works, its benefits, and how to use it to their advantage. This approach is further reinforced by trainers or managers who show the employees how to read feedback reports and who address other critical issues on an individual basis. This approach of implementing a plan gradually, from a capped to an aggressive gain-sharing or incentive plan, has usually been well received, both by senior executives and affected employees. It offers the ability to test the system, become adjusted to it, and work out any initial operational problems.

❏ HOW MUCH INCENTIVE TO PAY

Most banks feel comfortable offering their employees the opportunity to earn between 7.5 to 15 percent of their base salaries, if they perform considerably better than average. As the bank becomes accustomed to incentives and refines the process, potential earnings of 15 to 30 percent of base salaries (excluding promotionals) are not uncommon. Base salaries are often frozen or are adjusted only for inflation, once the employees are accustomed to an incentive system. Even a 25 to 30 percent increase equates to approximately 15 percent above the market's average pay for similar positions, and is only paid out for superior performance. Surveys indicate little relationship between base salaries and performance levels. Paying less in base salary but more in incentive pay will reward the bank's top performers.

Incentive pay should also be heavily based on profitability, not volume. For this reason, a strong attempt should be made to quantify the profitability of each product or account. This will ensure that the incentive payout is for sales that were profitable for the bank and met senior management strategy. To ensure that both of these objectives are achieved, several banks weight their products and services against profitability and "fit" with management goals. Establishing a weighting process also assists in deciding how much incentive to pay out for the products or services sold.

❑ PROVIDING FEEDBACK WITH INCENTIVES

A key to the success of any incentive program is the inclusion of feedback along with the incentive payout. This is crucial to per-ceptually linking pay with performance, so that employees are motivated to repeat the behavior. Participants must also know exactly where they stand in comparison with their peers. The feedback report should state explicitly why the employee is re-ceiving the check (by accounts, dates, and volumes), and a con-gratulatory note should be included.

Written statements frequently accompany the feedback re-ports, reminding employees that customers are both the rea-son for and the source of the incentive pay. Employees who do not receive incentives in a given period should also receive reports. All reports should specify current performance and the threshold level needed to earn incentives.

❑ METHOD OF INCENTIVE PAYOUT

Incentive rewards should be paid out in check or cash rather than by direct deposit. In addition, incentive payout should not be made on the same day as the payroll, so that its impact is increased. It should ideally be handed out at the end of each monthly or bi-weekly sales meeting. This reinforces the associa-tion of sales with additional pay, emphasizes the importance of sales meetings, and adds an extra boost to employee morale immediately following each sales meeting.

Most banks have discovered that, if the incentive pay fluctuates greatly from one period to the next, incentives tend to be more effective in the long run; if it remains consistent, it ceases to reward and encourage improved performance between periods. A threshold policy will tend to increase incentive pay fluctuation.

❏ TIMING OF PAYOUT

The sooner incentives can be paid after a sale is made, the more effective they become in modifying employee behavior. Monthly payout is common for administrative reasons and to ensure a motivational incentive accumulation amount. To maximize effectiveness, several banks shorten the incentive measurement period from a monthly or quarterly cycle to a 1- or 2-week cycle, with payout 2 days after the cycle ends.

For officers whose incentive is lending volume, banks frequently withhold loan incentives for an extended period of time, to ensure loan quality and profitability. To motivate these lenders, some banks initially pay out 50 to 75 percent of expected incentive. Once the exact quality of the loan is determined, the remainder of the incentive is calculated and paid out. Other banks pay out immediately, basing incentives on potential profitability, adjusted by a risk factor decided on by a credit committee, or through credit scoring. This last method provides an immediate incentive for high-quality loans and no incentive for marginal or poor-quality loans.

Contrary to common opinion that small incentive payout in any given period leads to negative reinforcement, a number of banks report that small incentives have a strong positive effect on performance. As a result, they have dropped minimum payout policies.

10

Improving Sales *and* Service

A high-performance sales culture is dependent on a strong service culture. Customer satisfaction and retention are critical to increased market share and individual customer profitability.

◻ IMPORTANCE OF SERVICE QUALITY

Because of the costs of initial account acquisition and processing, banks often do not realize a profit from customers until well into the relationship. Most products become increasingly profitable, the longer customers are kept. Long-term customer loyalty allows banks to charge a premium for services, further bolstering product profitability in later years. Figure 10–1 illustrates customer profitability over time. Banks with lower defection rates and higher degrees of customer loyalty can yield even better financial results than banks with substantially lower product costs and greater market share. A 2 percent decrease in defection rates is the financial equivalent of a 10 percent decrease in product cost at a given point, as illustrated in Figure 10–1. A sustainable competitive advantage strategy based on both building a sales culture and lowering defection rates can overwhelm strategies based on lower costs. Investment in improved service quality is crucial to a

BANK CARD INDUSTRY EXAMPLE

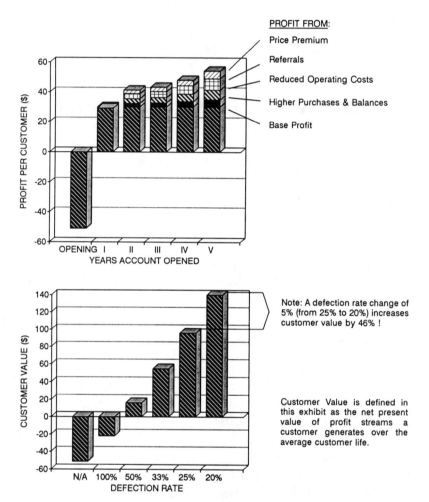

Figure 10-1 Customer Profitability over Time (Adapted from: Reichheld, F., and Sasser, W. "Zero Defections: Quality Comes to Services" *Harvard Business Review*, Sept.–Oct. 1990: 105–111.)

successful sales culture, in terms of increased margins and overall profitability.

☐ MEASURING RELATIONSHIP DEFECTION

One of the most useful benchmarks a bank can use to measure and improve service quality is defection analysis. By studying why customers close certain accounts or end relationships entirely, a bank can gain valuable insight into which service aspects are meaningful to the customer and which are not worth improving. By identifying trends early, a bank can improve specific services before being seriously hurt. Most high-performance banks have established standard operating procedures that ensure that defection feedback and analysis results are quickly and continuously relayed and acted on by senior management. When properly used, defection analysis provides management with a powerful tool that can be used to improve the quality of relevant services.

☐ THRESHOLDS OF SERVICE RECOVERY EXCELLENCE

Despite service quality training, reinforcement, and diligent follow-up, service failures will still occur, although at a much reduced frequency. All employees should be trained and expected to expertly handle service recovery. Most customers expect a certain level of service. When a service quality accident occurs, merely correcting the problem in a reasonable time frame is not the solution. Even if the problem is corrected, the customer realizes the mistake never should have happened and will be either indifferent or negative about the service received. Service recovery in its most effective form means doing something for the customer beyond what is anticipated. This high level of service recovery breaks through the customer's expected service range threshold and is perceived by the customer as excellence in customer service. Every bank should establish a service recovery goal aimed at piercing the customer's perceived *service excellence threshold.*

In establishing a service recovery system, a bank must modify its service delivery system to handle exceptions as routine. When accidents do happen, employees must know immediately what corrective action to take or they will simply reinforce the customer's dissatisfaction. In other words, standard operating procedures should include the flexibility to handle problems as routine events.

Proper service recovery procedures must include communicating to the customer exactly what actions were taken to resolve the problem in a timely manner. Even if a problem cannot be solved, the customer should be told the reason why.

❏ BUILDING QUALITY SERVICE CIRCLES

A number of banks have established special customer retention and quality service committees that examine probable reasons for defection, carefully analyze defection data, and make recommendations to senior management on organization, process, and job changes that eliminate or reduce customer defections and increase service levels. In some banks, the quality service committee function is part of the sales advisory committee's duties (described in Chapter 2). Retaining existing customers is essential to increasing market share and profitability in highly competitive markets.

❏ SERVICE QUALITY PROGRAM POSITIONING

A primary obstacle to service quality program effectiveness is employee rejection. Most employees feel that they already provide the best service possible and do not feel that a service quality program will substantially increase the existing level of service. Several banks have addressed this problem by positioning their service quality programs as elitist programs in which excellence is expected but dazzling performance is commendable. Altering employee perceptions of what constitutes excellent service is critical.

❏ REWARDING INTERNAL SERVICE QUALITY

Employees without direct customer contact often have a substantial effect on a bank's sales culture. These employees can be effectively encouraged to deliver excellent service to their internal clients through incentives. For example, in banks that have decreased line lending authority to implement aggressive incentives without portfolio quality deterioration, relationship managers and branch managers become increasingly dependent on the credit area for timely loan approvals. Some banks have paid credit analysts and managers incentives based on turnaround time, in conjunction with total portfolio profitability. The incentives do not penalize credit analysts for rejecting loan requests and therefore they avoid placing pressure on approving marginal loans. Because these incentives reward analysts for loan portfolio profitability, proper analysis and loan quality are encouraged. These reward principles can be applied to many other areas of the bank, to increase service performance. Qualified employees can be rewarded based on turnaround time, quality of services, operations efficiency, expense containment, and evaluation results by their internal clients.

❏ EMPOWERING AT ALL LEVELS

Few problems anger retail or wholesale customers more than having a bank employee inform them that the authority to solve a problem is provided by someone else. Employees who deal with customers on a daily basis are in the best position to know what service or sales problems exist and which customers are dissatisfied. Customers do not want to wait for their problems to filter through various organizational and departmental levels before a satisfactory resolution is reached. The front line must be able to identify service and sales problems and empowered to resolve them.

Empowerment means providing employees with the authority, responsibility, and incentives to follow through on a problem, from identification to successful conclusion. Authority means that employees can investigate problems, correct them, credit accounts, send gifts or premiums, and make decisions that directly solve the customer's problems. Responsibility means that employees both recognize the need and feel obligated to *act* and resolve customer problems, not just to accept the blame, as a regular and routine part of their jobs. Lastly, employees must be given incentives for their accountability, proficiency, and service recovery. Service recovery should be a factor taken into consideration when employees are evaluated for future promotions and pay raises. A number of banks take this last step further, by providing cash or stock incentives for successful service recovery. Recognition and premiums, such as quality service pins, are commonplace in most high-performance banks.

❑ SERVICE GUARANTEES

A number of banks back up their service quality claims with service guarantees. If a retail customer is not satisfied with the bank's service for any reason, then that customer is compensated for the dissatisfaction. Some adjustments made for customers include small payments of cash or credit, waiver of monthly or yearly service charges, gifts, dinner certificates, and tickets to sporting events and shows. Several banks extend their service guarantees to include wait-time thresholds. If a customer waits longer than a certain specified time (often 5 to 7 minutes), the customer is compensated. In addition, a few banks have credit pools for branches, departments, or even individual employees. When customer adjustments are lower than the credit pool's contents, the remainder of the pool is distributed to the employees. Shared pools motivate all employees to excel and reward them for doing so.

❑ SERVICE PLEDGES

Service pledges are becoming common as quality service programs advance. Service pledges outline the basic commitments to service that all bank employees are expected to meet or exceed. With proper implementation, these pledges become part of a bank's corporate values and are discussed in initial employee training. Service pledges can include:

- "Sundown Rule"—all customer problems and concerns should be resolved on the same day. If more time is needed, the customer should be contacted on the same day with an explanation of why more time is needed and what steps are being taken to get the problem resolved.
- All phone calls should be answered in four rings or less.
- All phone calls should be returned on the same day.

❏ ENABLING CUSTOMERS TO REWARD TOP PERFORMERS

Service quality is irrelevant unless perceived to be of value to the customer. A few banks determine which employees provide top quality service by involving customers in service quality incentives. Once or twice each year, a token or poker chip is mailed out to every bank customer with a note requesting that the customer give the tokens to the employees who have provided the best service. The employees use the accumulated tokens to earn prizes, merchandise, and other incentives. An example of one bank's program follows:

Loyal (and profitable) customers have always been the product of good relationships and excellent service. Our bank sought to reward employees who built solid relationships and provided top service. However, we were not satisfied with service audits, customer questionnaires, and other conventional methods. In many cases (if not the majority), our retail customers knew our employees' faces but not their names—making questionnaires inaccurate in identifying our best service providers. In other cases, our customers felt that surveys and questionnaires never made a direct difference and most customers would not respond. We needed a new and long-term method of measuring quality service and relationship building.

We had previously seen poker chips used in quality service programs in the hotel industry and we decided to adapt the strategy for use within our bank. Throughout each year, customer mailings consisting of a poker chip and a note are now sent out. The note contains a brief explanation of the bank's service quality goals and incentive program based on the poker chips (embossed with the bank's insignia). Customers are encouraged to pass the chips along to the bank employee who has provided top quality service to them. The mailings are sent throughout the year and are balanced out evenly by weeks. Each customer receives a chip twice a year. This allows us to run a continuous and measurable service quality program. Weekly and monthly contests are held throughout the year by branch and region. The program has been an incredible success at the bank, ensuring that our representatives are always at their very best!

❏ VISUAL COMMITMENTS OF SERVICE EXCELLENCE

A statement of a bank's commitment to service excellence is often prominently displayed at the entrance of a department or branch. It may contain the department or branch manager's name and signature, as a gesture of the manager's commitment to service quality. These visual commitment symbols are effective in ensuring a dedication to service quality, from senior management down.

❏ ESTABLISHING DISCRETIONARY POLICIES

Policies often inconvenience customers. Most banks instruct their line employees to follow all policies and then have managers sign off for any exceptions. This leads to inconsistent application of policies between areas, and customer delays each time a manager's signature is needed.

Several banks formalize the exceptions process by establishing policy priorities. Certain policies are color-coded to indicate that they are never to be waived. Others can be waived or modified, depending on specified requirements or conditions. Still others may be waived according to the employee's judgment. The prioritizing of policies leads to a more consistent treatment throughout the bank. Prioritizing also speeds customer service and ensures that the bank's top customers are treated well by empowering all employees to make prudent business decisions.

❏ NEVER SAYING NO

Few things infuriate customers more, or cause more customer ill will, than the response "No." Employees should be trained to tell customers "Yes, if . . ." in most cases. When coaching and role playing are provided, employees can be trained to relay to customers the criteria that would allow the bank to grant a customer's request. To establish a "never say no" policy and still uphold both prudent and stringent credit quality standards, takes training and commitment.

❏ MEETING CUSTOMER WAIT-TIME THRESHOLDS

Providing excellent service means delivery in a time frame that seems fair and reasonable to the *customer*. Time, from a customer's perspective, often has little in common with factors measured by banks. Some customers will be aggravated at having to wait for 10 seconds, if they perceive that the bank staff is involved in "horseplay" or otherwise purposefully not being receptive. Similarly, a customer could potentially wait over 5 minutes, yet still be satisfied with service during peak periods when it appears that all employees are doing their very best to provide timely service. A threshold level of customer expectancy is dependent on a number of factors:

- Time of day
- Day of the month
- Previous experience at the specific location
- Time available
- Mood and disposition
- Perception of the bank's willingness to provide timely service.

Although banks cannot address personal factors, they can address all other variables. The bank's primary task is not to provide a certain average wait-time across all branches, but rather to identify what threshold levels of service customers expect at certain times, locations, and days. Because customer expectancy can only be determined by getting customer feedback, determining threshold levels involves getting immediate feedback by distributing questionnaires while the customer is being served, or by having market researchers outside the facility question customers as they are leaving. Once the data are collected and analyzed, management will be able to determine the approximate wait-time thresholds that must be met at each location by time and day, to compare this information to each location's historical activity records by time and day, and to staff accordingly.

The bank's secondary task is to train employees to ensure that customers perceive that their needs are being responded to. On the retail side, these actions include:

- Counting money or proofing work out of sight of customers. Customers expect that "all hands should be on deck." Most customers become annoyed when they observe employees performing tasks other than directly assisting customers.

- Avoiding discussions on phones, or among employees, while customers are waiting or being served. Because customers cannot hear or understand telephone or personal conversations, they assume that the employees are ignoring their needs, regardless of whether the discussions are of a business nature.

- Acknowledging the customer's presence as soon as the customer begins to wait, especially if there is no formalized line or waiting system. Platform representatives should acknowledge a customer who begins to wait while another is being served and phone procedures should require that customers are served in the order called.

❑ REDUCING WAIT-TIME PERCEPTION

Customer wait-time thresholds can be influenced by altering customer perception of time. By adjusting the customers' surroundings and environmental factors, several banks have taken nontraditional steps to reduce the perception of waiting time. A leading bank described its approach this way:

> One successful technique we have implemented at our higher-volume branches is the suspension of television sets from the ceiling, behind the teller windows. Depending on the branch manager's preference, the televisions are either set on a 24-hour news station, or continuous videos of various retail bank products are run. The television sets are on only during peak periods of extremely busy days. Our branch surveys indicate that customers exposed to the television entertainment become noticeably less sensitive to the waiting time they endure and that overall customer satisfaction has increased.

Some banks exhibit art work and sculptures near teller lines. Again, by distracting customers from thinking about waiting time, dissatisfaction is reduced.

❏ EXPRESS TELLER LANES

A retail store adaptation introduced successfully by many banks is the *express teller lane* for noncommercial customers who have only one transaction. At some banks, even more restrictions apply, such as no money orders. The express lanes not only satisfy customers who simply want to perform a quick transaction, but also frequently provide the Marketing Department with great ammunition for use in their retail advertisements.

❏ FLEXIBLE INTEREST RATES

In recognition of different margin contributions made by each customer, several banks have empowered their branch managers and platform representatives to negotiate rates on both loans and deposits. By controlling the spread allowance and requiring a certain average interest rate, these banks avoid losing price-sensitive customers, yet they maximize revenues from those customers who are not price-sensitive. Allowing employees to administer flexible rates ensures that discounts or premiums are not paid to customers unnecessarily. The size and depth of the banking relationship are frequently taken into consideration when deciding on flexible loan and deposit rates.

❏ SUPERMARKET BRANCHES

One concept not yet widely implemented is the partial-service *supermarket branch*. By situating a mini-branch within a supermarket, many banks have tactfully placed their resources in a location where there is strong traffic flow of both existing customers and prospects. At approximately one-fifth of the cost of a brick-and-mortar building, supermarket branches have lower overhead costs and can be staffed by a skeleton crew, to maximize efficiency.

The most successful supermarket branches are in supermarkets that have large amounts of square footage and heavy traffic flow. An extra employee often works the aisles, to bring in new business. The branches rarely do the supermarket's own banking since this would require unwanted personnel overhead, to handle both the unsteady and high-cash processing demands of a supermarket, in addition to serving the bank's customers. The low personnel overhead needed to operate a supermarket branch allows extended banking hours and Saturday banking at a minimal cost. Some banks have *reduced* hours of service at regular facilities with lower traffic flows by referring customers who need extended hours to the supermarket branches. Here is a top bank's strategy to protect its location advantage:

> In order to ensure that we preserve our location advantages over other competitors, we have negotiated renewable "options" to tentatively locate either branches or automatic teller machines in strategic supermarket and retail store sites at a future date. For a relatively modest price, we have contractually locked out our competitors from key facilities and assured ourselves a location, should we later decide to open a supermarket branch, store branch, or automatic teller machine at one of these strategic sites.

❏ TELEPHONE SERVICE CENTERS

Different from normal customer service lines, *telephone service centers* (or *telebanking centers*) are designed to move a large portion of account servicing away from high-overhead branch systems. One of the primary differences between telebanking centers and normal customer service lines is that customers cannot place any direct telephone calls to a branch. When customers call the bank, all lines are routed to the telebanking center. Only during emergencies are calls allowed to pass through to the branches.

By shifting away some servicing activities, telebanking centers allow platform representatives and branch managers the time needed to focus on both selling and business development. In addition, telebanking centers allow branch employees to provide improved relationship banking to customers who prefer to meet them face-to-face. Telebanking centers can also be easily converted to outbound telephone sales centers.

Wholesale banking is rapidly becoming a commodity business. In an attempt to offer superior service, several banks offer wholesale customers the ability to contact business telebanking centers. Although difficulties have been encountered in providing qualified staff to deal with complex wholesale products and problems, these centers nonetheless provide another channel of service delivery.

❏ ESTABLISHING COMPLAINT LINES

Surveys indicate that most customers will not express their dissatisfaction with a bank before leaving for another institution. Service problems must therefore be resolved before they cause customer indifference or alienation. Dedicated toll-free complaint lines provide an avenue for customers to resolve service problems quickly and effortlessly. Because there is increased retention of disgruntled customers, complaint lines quickly pay for themselves.

Complaint lines are usually staffed by the bank's most skilled customer service representatives. These representatives are empowered with a small arsenal of tools and the authority to take action and retain customers. In turn, they are rewarded for both retaining customers and cross-selling products based on customer needs. For example, if a customer calls to complain about a bank mistake that led to an overdraft, the service representatives correct the bank's error and then suggest an overdraft protection credit line. In the event that the overdraft was not the bank's fault, the service representative could offer to waive the overdraft fee if the customer accepts the credit line.

Branches at some progressive banks are equipped with clearly visible telephone hotlines that connect customers directly to the dedicated complaint line. This hotline serves as an overflow device when all branch platform representatives are occupied and a customer has an urgent request or problem. There are also numerous applications on the wholesale side.

11

Summary

Much attention has been paid to the steps and tools that are useful in building a high-performance sales culture. In most banks, however, lasting organizational change has been elusive, even when actionable goals and objectives are well defined. High-performance banks have methods for effecting *lasting* organizational change.

Most companywide programs for change that are directed from the top, or from corporate areas such as Human Resources or Marketing, have historically been ineffective in both duration and effect (Beer, Eisenstat, and Spector, 1990). Most long-term and effective corporate change programs are launched from the grass-roots level. Line and department managers are the key to corporate change.

The challenges lie in mobilizing commitment by line and department managers, in developing a shared vision and consensus for the new sales culture, and in providing the necessary tools and support as line and department managers implement and lead the changes. Although logical, this strategy directly conflicts with many senior managers' preconceptions that top-down hierarchy should be the primary method of organizational management. Overcoming this preconception is one of the most difficult challenges most senior managers face, in realizing effective organizational change.

To ensure lasting advancement in a bank's sales culture, the individuals providing the impetus must view themselves as catalysts of change—regardless of whether they are part of senior management; or responsible for marketing, sales management, or line management; or heads of departments. They must explain the ultimate goals, receive buy-in, ask for open-ended action, and then provide the necessary support, guidance, rewards, and recognition to the respective line managers and department heads who will lead the culture change. Sometimes it is preferable to allow each department and line manager to reinvent the wheel, if the result is individual ownership of the actions and goals. The cultural change formula is summarized as follows:

- *Explain the goals.* By meeting with all managers within each targeted department or region, senior management can discuss past and existing barriers to increased profitability.

- *Receive buy-in.* Once consensus is reached about the causes, the idea of a second-generation sales culture should be introduced and discussed in terms of viability and long-term effectiveness. The ultimate goal of this exercise is to receive buy-in with as many managers within the targeted department or area as possible.

- *Ask for open-ended action.* Expect the department's or area's managers to take the initiative. Ask for commitment, and jointly set crude goals that can be refined as the managers gain experience in developing the sales culture in their areas.

- *Provide the necessary support and guidance.* Once consensus and commitment are reached, timely training and experience sharing are critical, in order to provide the tools, expertise, and capability needed by each of the managers to pursue the agreed-on goals.

- *Reward and recognize.* Cohesion and momentum should be fostered by constant encouragement and by sharing and

rewarding all successes. Recognition of successes throughout the bank is critical to encouraging change in departments and areas that have not yet begun the sales culture
evolution.

Most banks that have successfully achieved a lasting sales
culture work from the periphery inward. In sharp contrast to
bankwide efforts directed from the center and involving every
department and area at once, specific departments or regions
with the highest probability of success should be chosen to lead
the undertaking. These departments or areas can be used as
positive examples and champions, once they begin to demonstrate positive gains. It is then possible for bank management to
leverage these gains, to create synergy and momentum in other
areas. This is not to say that centrally-directed bankwide efforts
cannot succeed, but the chances of lasting success are too un-
predictable to pursue as a corporate strategy in most banks.

A checklist of selected ideas is shown in Table 11–1.

Building a second-generation sales culture does not involve
simply providing sales training, incentives, automation, or other
"quick fix" solutions. Rather, building a high-performance sales
culture involves the implementation of continuous short-cycle
innovations and improvements, with each being complementary
to the next.

W. Edwards Deming, frequently credited by Japanese busi-
nesspeople for management techniques that revitalized their industrial base from postwar devastation to modern-day promi-
nence, frequently emphasized the importance of continual
improvement. Is the Marketing Department more effective this
year than last? Are the bank's front-line employees better able to
sell the bank's services today than they were 3 months ago?
Citing a goal is useless, according to Deming, unless management has a method for reaching the goal. Continuous improvement is this method.

Figure 11–1 shows a *sales culture life cycle*. Each sales innovation or improvement is shown by a solid line. Initial sales culture
improvements, taken individually, are brief in duration and have
a minimal effect on overall bank profitability. Each incremental

Table 11-1 Sales Culture Construction Checklist

Senior Management Checklist

1. ____ Establish a sales leadership committee to spearhead the implementation of a sales culture.

2. ____ Form a sales barrier reduction task force to reduce sales inefficiencies and obstructions.

3. ____ Establish and participate in bankwide sales management meetings for planning and sales support.

4. ____ Assist in the establishment and backing of a sales support manager and other sales positions.

5. ____ Be directly involved in the rewarding and recognition of top sales performers throughout the bank.

6. ____ Lead all new sales campaigns and efforts by first announcement and active participation.

7. ____ Encourage upbeat sales competition among divisions, departments, and branches.

8. ____ Praise top-performing divisions, departments, or branches, and frequently cite them as examples.

9. ____ Flatten the organization by redefining mid-management roles to include partial sales responsibilities.

10. ____ Separate operations and sales duties, to allow line officers to concentrate on sales and sales management.

11. ____ Tier sales positions to allow advancement and progression of line employees with sales responsibility.

12. ____ Establish a sales and sales management career track within each department of the bank.

13. ____ Separate lending authority and business development functions to ensure strong credit standards.

Table 11–1 (*continued*)

14. ____ Establish high-value customer programs in all departments, to increase retention and relationship depth.

15. ____ Establish a service recovery system and quality service circles, and assign defections goals to the line.

16. ____ Empower the Human Resources area to administer validated sales screening tests to job applicants.

17. ____ Establish sales certification for employee advancement in positions that include sales responsibilities.

18. ____ Mandate the creation of on-the-job development plans for each employee to include sales skills.

19. ____ Be present at and launch the opening of all sales and sales management training sessions.

20. ____ Commission a sales performers' club to recognize the bank's top sales achievers.

Department/Branch/Sales Manager Checklist

1. ____ Jointly develop a list of key accounts, retention goals, and account strategies with each employee.

2. ____ Encourage joint calls, evaluate all aspects of each call, and then provide detailed feedback.

3. ____ Set time aside each day for sales management and coaching of employees without interruptions.

4. ____ Encourage upbeat sales competition among employees; reward top performers weekly.

5. ____ Redefine employee responsibilities to increase available sales time and reduce administrative time.

6. ____ Identify and realign the department's most capable relationship managers with its key customers.

Table 11-1   (*continued*)

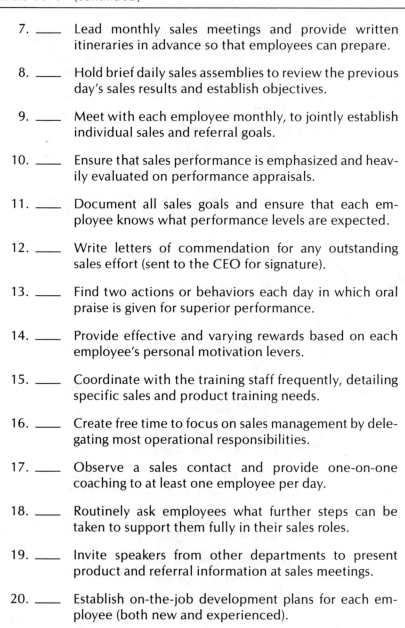

7. ____ Lead monthly sales meetings and provide written itineraries in advance so that employees can prepare.

8. ____ Hold brief daily sales assemblies to review the previous day's sales results and establish objectives.

9. ____ Meet with each employee monthly, to jointly establish individual sales and referral goals.

10. ____ Ensure that sales performance is emphasized and heavily evaluated on performance appraisals.

11. ____ Document all sales goals and ensure that each employee knows what performance levels are expected.

12. ____ Write letters of commendation for any outstanding sales effort (sent to the CEO for signature).

13. ____ Find two actions or behaviors each day in which oral praise is given for superior performance.

14. ____ Provide effective and varying rewards based on each employee's personal motivation levers.

15. ____ Coordinate with the training staff frequently, detailing specific sales and product training needs.

16. ____ Create free time to focus on sales management by delegating most operational responsibilities.

17. ____ Observe a sales contact and provide one-on-one coaching to at least one employee per day.

18. ____ Routinely ask employees what further steps can be taken to support them fully in their sales roles.

19. ____ Invite speakers from other departments to present product and referral information at sales meetings.

20. ____ Establish on-the-job development plans for each employee (both new and experienced).

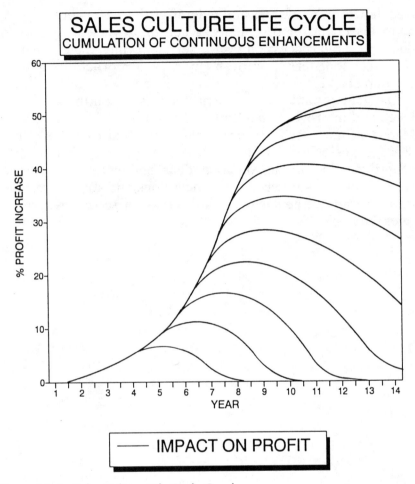

Figure 11–1 Sales Culture Life Cycle Graph

step, however, reinforces and magnifies the effects of foregoing and subsequent improvements. When improvements are introduced in rapid succession over a period of time, the cumulative effect is a long-term improvement in bank profitability and the buildup of a high-performance, second-generation sales culture.

The goal of bank management, then, is to continuously challenge and improve its bank in terms of both sales and service. Managers must strive to break the mold that casts them into average performers by never leaving well enough alone, by adapting and improving on good ideas, and by continuous innovation. Only by shattering preconceptions and striving for continuous improvement can a bank create a second-generation sales culture.

References and Suggested Readings

Abernathy, W. *Designing and Managing an Organization-Wide Incentive Pay System.* Memphis, TN: W. B. Abernathy & Assoc., 1990.

Arahood, Dale A. *Incentive Compensation Plan Workbook.* Rolling Meadows, IL: Bank Administration Institute, 1984.

Beer, M., Eisenstat, R., and Spector, B. "Why Change Programs Don't Produce Change." *Harvard Business Review* (November–December 1990): 158–166.

Berry, L., Bennett, D., and Brown, C. *Service Quality.* Homewood, IL: Dow Jones-Irwin, 1989.

Berry, L., Futrell, C., and Bowers, M. *Bankers Who Sell.* Homewood, IL: Dow Jones-Irwin, 1985.

Bettinger, Cass. "The Nine Principles of War." *Bank Marketing* (December 1989): 33–34.

Bhide, Amar. "Hustle as Strategy." *Harvard Business Review* (September–October 1986): 59–65.

Boothe, W., and Kikta, J. "Developing a Sales Culture: One Bank's Success." *The Bankers Magazine* (March–April, 1989): 32–36.

Bragg, A. "Are Good Salespeople Born or Made?" *Sales & Marketing Management* (September, 1988): 74–78.

Brennan, Leslie. "Getting a New Incentive Program Off the Ground." *Sales & Marketing Management* (May 1989): 74–79.

———. "Promoting Quality Sales Through Incentives." *Sales & Marketing Management* (May 1989): 65–67.

Buckingham, William A. "A Winning Strategy for Branch Banking." *The Bankers Magazine* (May–June, 1988): 14–18.

Burt, Bradley L. "Focusing the Private Banking Unit for Results." *Private Banking* (Summer 1989): 21–24.

Butler, L., and Dynan, F. "Putting Service Quality into Practice: A Case Study." *Journal of Retail Banking* (Winter 1988–1989): 5–13.

Cooper, Charles R. *The Process of Creating and Sustaining a Retail Bank Sales Culture.* Master's thesis, University of Delaware, Newark DE, 1987.

Cortis, John. "Why Boutique Private Banks Can Take on the Big Boys—and Win." *Private Banking* (Summer 1990): 13–18.

Corwin, Scott L. "How to Discover People Who Have What It Takes to Sell." *Bank Marketing* (November 1987): 10–12.

Council on Financial Competition. *Deepening Customer Relations: Relationship Pricing.* Washington, DC: The Advisory Board, 1988.

———. *Defining Excellence in Middle Market Lending: Analysis.* Washington, DC: The Advisory Board 1989.

———. *Excellence in Branch Banking III: Retail Sales Incentives.* Washington, DC: The Advisory Board, 1988.

———. *Financial Service Telemarketing to Mid-Size Companies.* Washington, DC: The Advisory Board, 1985.

———. *Managing for Excellence in Cash Management Sales.* Washington, DC: The Advisory Board, 1990.

———. *New Products and Services for Small Business.* Washington, DC: The Advisory Board, 1990.

————. *19 Alternative Tactics for Selling Investment Products.* Washington, DC: The Advisory Board, 1989.

————. *Profit Strategies for the Middle Market.* Washington, DC: The Advisory Board, 1986.

————. *Retail Excellence II: Aggressive Branch Sales.* Washington, DC: The Advisory Board, 1987.

————. *Retail Selling: Reorganization and Incentive Compensation.* Washington, DC: The Advisory Board, 1984.

————. *Transforming Calling Officer Performance through Incentives.* Washington, DC: The Advisory Board, 1989.

Cranfill, S. "Profitably Banking the Small Business." *Journal of Commercial Bank Lending* (October 1990): 38–44.

Crigger, Jerry W. "Corporate Management Training—A Fresh Approach." *Loan Training,* 85–94. Philadelphia: RMA, 1990.

Crill, Linda S. "Five Steps Toward Developing a Winning . . . Team." *Private Banking* (Winter 1989): 30–33.

Darby, Lawrence A. "Better Training: The Key to Better Banking." *Loan Training,* 9–14. Philadelphia: RMA, 1990.

Dennis, William J. "Competing for the Small Business Market." *The Bankers Magazine* (May–June, 1989): 34–39.

Dibbert, Michael T. "Selling Non-Traditional Investment Products." *The Bankers Magazine* (March–April, 1988): 52–59.

Donnelly, J., Berry, L. and Thompson, T. *Marketing Financial Services.* Homewood, IL: Dow Jones-Irwin, 1985.

Donnelly, James H., and Skinner, Steven J. *The New Banker.* Homewood, IL: Dow Jones-Irwin, 1989.

Fallar, Jaye E. "Incentive Compensation Programs That Really Work." *Private Banking* (Summer 1988): 15–17.

Falvey, Jack. "It's Loyalty That Binds the Sales Force Together." *Sales & Marketing Management* (July 1989): 24–25.

Fink, Ronald B. "Banks Get Serious About Sales Training." *U.S. Banker* (September 1990): 49–52.

Finkin, Eugene. "Company Turnaround." *Journal of Business Strategy* (Spring 1985): 14–25.

Furlong, Carla B. "Customer Service is More Than Just Talk." *Bank Marketing* (May 1990): 37–39.

———. *Marketing Money*. Chicago: Probus Publishing Co., 1989.

German, Donald R., and German, Joan W. *Tested Techniques in Bank Marketing*. Boston: Warren, Gorham & Lamont, 1978.

Ghemawat, Pankaj. "Sustainable Advantage." *Harvard Business Review* (September–October 1986): 53–58.

Goodman, J., Burke, M., and Grimm, C. "How to Determine Whether Your Customers. . . ." *Private Banking* (Summer 1990): 7–12.

Grden-Elison, Nancy. "Cash-less Incentives—Another Way to Reward Performance." *Bank Marketing* (July 1987): 14–17.

Gurney, Peter. "Wait a Minute!" *Bank Marketing* (April 1990): 37–39.

Hanan, Mack. *Consultative Selling*, 3rd ed. New York: AMACOM: 1985.

Handel, William, *Strategic Marketing: Senior Management Perspective*. Austin, TX: Sheshunoff Information Services, 1989.

Hayden, Catherine. *The Handbook of Strategic Expertise*. New York: Free Press, 1986.

Hendrickson, John. "Training in Context." *Training* (March 1990): 65–70.

Hersh, Anita K. "Monthly Statements Trumpet Relationship Era." *Bank Marketing* (December 1987): 30–31.

Hinkle, C., and Alexander, B. "Direct Mail: Targeting for Results." *Journal of Retail Banking* (Spring 1988): 31–38.

Hofer, C. "Turnaround Strategies." *Journal of Business Strategy* (Summer 1980): 19–31.

Hubbard, Jack. "How to Make Better Sales Calls." *ABA Banking Journal* (October 1988): 78–82.

Hudson, P., and Swanick, R. *Sales Management for Retail Bankers*. Austin, TX: Sheshunoff Information Services, 1989.

Jewett, Walter G., and Guss, Jonathan S. G. "Calling Force Management and . . ." *Loan Training*, 95–103, Philadelphia: RMA, 1990.

Kotler, Phillip. *Marketing Management: Analysis, Planning, and Control.* Englewood Cliffs, NJ: Prentice-Hall, 1976.

———. *Marketing Professional Services.* Englewood Cliffs, NJ: Prentice-Hall, 1984.

Lee, Chris. "Talking Back to the Boss." *Training* (April 1990): 29–35.

Littlewood, Shain & Co. *Measuring the Relationship Profitability . . .*" Rolling Meadows, IL: BAI, 1988.

Long, Robert H. "High Performance Bank Culture." *Journal of Retail Banking* (Fall 1988): 13–22.

Mauney, G., and Conway, J. "Here Comes the Private Banking Data Base." *Private Banking* (Winter 1988): 31–35.

McIver, C., and Naylor, G. *Marketing Financial Services.* London: The Institute of Bankers, 1980.

McCormack, Mark H. *What They Don't Teach You at Harvard Business School.* New York: Bantam Books, 1986.

Meenan, Peter. "Are Mutual Funds in Your Future?" *ABA Banking Journal* (April 1990): 47–51.

Meidan, Arthur. *Bank Marketing Management.* London: Macmillan Publishers, 1984.

Mellow, Craig. "The Best Source of Competitive Intelligence." *Sales & Marketing Management* (December 1989): 24–29.

Miller, Arthur R. *Selling Financial Services.* Rolling Meadows, IL: BAI: 1987.

Miller, Arthur R., and Nesbit, Robert G. "How Does Your Bank Score on This Culture Test?" *Bank Marketing* (March 1986): 10–14.

Miller, Robert B., and Heiman, Stephen E. *Strategic Selling.* New York: William Morrow and Co., 1985.

Miner, L., and Zemke, S. "Cross-Selling Training with Bottom-Line Results." *Bank Marketing* (December 1989): 25–26.

Mirabile, Richard J. "The Power of Job Analysis." *Training* (April 1990): 70–74.

Moriarty, R., and Moran, U. "Managing Hybrid Marketing Systems." *Harvard Business Review* (November–December 1990): 146–155.

——— and Swartz, G. "Automation to Boost Sales and Marketing." *Harvard Business Review* (January–February 1989): 100–108.

Palmer, David R. "Three Ways to Increase Private Banker Productivity." *Private Banking* (Summer 1989): 11–14.

———. "Turf Battles in Private Banking . . ." *Private Banking* (Winter 1988): 18–24.

Pennington, Judith A. *Creating a Sales Culture in a Community Bank.* Rolling Meadows, IL: BAI, 1988.

Peters, T. *In Search of Excellence.* New York: Warner Books, 1982.

———. *Thriving on Chaos.* New York: Harper & Row, 1987.

Porter, Michael E. "From Competitive Advantage to Corporate Strategy." *Harvard Business Review* (May–June 1987): 43–59.

———. Interview by Barry I. Deutsch. *Bank Marketing* (May 1990): 21–24.

Rackham, Neil. *Major Account Sales Strategy.* New York: McGraw-Hill, 1989.

———. *SPIN Selling.* New York: McGraw-Hill, 1988.

Rakow, Joel. "Not Just the Facts Ma'am." *Training* (June 1990): 59–61.

Reichheld, F., and Sasser, W. "Zero Defections: Quality Comes to Services." *Harvard Business Review* (September–October, 1990): 105–111.

Reidenbach, R. *Bank Marketing.* Englewood Cliffs, NJ: Prentice-Hall, 1986.

Richardson, L. *Bankers in the Selling Role.* New York: John Wiley & Sons, 1984.

Robinson, Dana G., and Robinson, J. *Training for Impact.* San Francisco: Jossey-Bass, 1989.

Robinson, L. "Role Playing as a Sales Training Tool." *Harvard Business Review* (May–June 1987): 34–38.

Rodgers, T. J. "No Excuses Management." *Harvard Business Review* (July–August 1990): 96–97.

Ross, J., and Kami, M. *Corporate Management in Crisis—Why the Mighty Fall.* Englewood Cliffs, NJ: Prentice-Hall, 1973.

SanFilippo, Barbara. "How to Energize Your Sales Staff." *Bank Marketing* (October 1988): 32–35.

———. "Personal Production Goals Boost Sales Output." *Bank Marketing* (August 1987): 6, 61.

Schuster, J., and Zingheim, P. "How Productivity-Based Pay Works . . ." *The Bankers Magazine* (May-June 1989): 62–66.

———. "Incentive Plans That Work." *ABA Banking Journal* (September 1988): 62–63.

Selwitz, Robert. "Blueprint for Performance Pay." *ABA Banking Journal* (May 1990): 18–20.

Shoultz, Donald. "Sales Incentives Withering at Many Banks." *American Banker* (March 1988): 2.

Simmons, R. D. "Bank Compensation in the Nineties." *U.S. Banker* (September 1990): 54–61.

Smith, Ivan C. *How to Analyze the Competition.* Boston: American Management Association, 1986.

Spadaford, J. "Attaining Service Excellence in Commercial Lending." *Journal of Commercial Bank Lending* (October 1990): 45–49.

Svare, J. C. "Forging Profitable Relationships." *Bank Administration* (November 1989): 14–24.

Tandy, G., and Stovel, R. "Are Your Branches Out on a Limb?" *Bank Marketing* (November 1989): 26–29.

Thompson, Thomas W. *Building a Selling Culture.* U.S. Banker, 1988.

van der Velde, Marjolijn. *Sales Incentive Programs for Branch Personnel.* Rolling Meadows, IL: BAI, 1987.

Whittle, Jack W. "Here's How to Rate Your Bank Marketing Efforts." *Bank Marketing* (June 1990): 40–42.

Zemke, R. *The Service Edge.* New York: New American Library, 1989.

Zimmerman, A. "Branch Managers, At Last, May Be . . ." *Bank Marketing* (April 1989): 26–28.

Index

BOOK REGISTRATION AND FEEDBACK

POWER BANKERS, by Michael F. Price

To receive notification of future editions, updates, related books, and supplements, return a photocopy of this registration page to the address below.

Name: _____

Title: _____

Bank/Co.: _____

Address: _____

City: _____ **State:** _____ **Zip/Postal Code:** _____

Country (Outside U.S.): _____ **Telephone:** _____

Comments: _____

_____

_____

_____

Enclose Additional Comments if Any

(Fold)

- -

**Affix
Stamp
Here**

**Michael F. Price
4950 Willeo Ridge Court
Marietta, GA 30068 USA**